unlocking the secret

the good life

lawrence powell

ARROWS & STONES

For foreign and subsidiary rights, contact the author.

Cover design by Sara Young
Cover photo by Andrew van Tilborgh

ISBN: 978-1-962401-32-6   1 2 3 4 5 6 7 8 9 10
Printed in the United States of America

WHAT PEOPLE ARE SAYING ABOUT
the good life

There are few persons who seem to have the zest for life that Larry Powell has; when you read this book, you will understand why he has it. *The Good Life* presents a guide for understanding the God-given plan for our lives that does indeed bring us "good success". Make sure you make this your next reading.

—Dr. Walter Scott Thomas, Sr.
New Psalmist Baptist Church
Baltimore, Maryland

I have been privileged to have been in relationship with Dr. Lawrence Powell for over twenty years. Ministry has taken me all around the world to over 1,500 churches in the United States alone. I can say unequivocally that Dr. Powell is one of the most prominent leaders in the body of Christ today! In his newest book, *The Good Life*, Dr. Powell gives the blueprint for how you can live a peaceful, happy, productive, and prosperous life! Let's stop pursuing what the world calls the good life and follow Dr. Powell's biblical instruction. We can have and obtain the life of abundance that Jesus brought to us in John 10:10! It is available now, and it is available for everyone! Thank you, Dr. Powell, for writing this book! It will transform all who read it, and it is one I will keep as a life book.

—Eric Smith
President, Smith Media Group

When solid theology, seasoned wisdom, and supernatural anointing come together to release healing and hope, you have something very rare and special. My friend, Dr. Lawrence Powell, has been providing healthy leadership training and creating relevant resources for God's people for decades. In *The Good Life*, he delivers once again. Here is a gift of pure gold that will inspire you, equip you, and lift you to the next level.

—Dr. David Cannistraci
Author of *Let's Talk About Teams* and *Apostles and the Emerging Apostolic Movement*
Lead Pastor of Gateway City Church
San Jose, California

Deep and wide. Relevant and reverent. *In The Good Life*, Dr. Lawrence Powell presents an easy-to-read deep dive into God's plan, purpose, and will for the reader. This book is an inspirational and motivational guide to understanding and receiving God's overflow ... His abundance into your life.

—Pastor John J. Wagner
Epic Church International

To Skylar—my heart and joy.
I love you always and forever.

CONTENTS

ACKNOWLEDGMENTS

To Jesus Christ, thanks for choosing me in spite of me. I'm forever grateful.

To the late Bishop Chandler David Owens, thanks for boosting my confidence and ordaining in me to serve in the LORD's Church.

Thanks a zillion to my Agape family. Your constant prayers, support, and encouragement are priceless. I am a better man and leader because of you.

Many thanks also to the following persons for being there for me through it all. I love and appreciate you more than you know and more than I can say.

Adria, Aaron, and Ashlyn Powell

Annette Gillette

Bishop Charles E. and Lady Mae Blake

Bishop Dale Bronner

Pastors Chandler and China Cleveland

Prophet Dennis Cramer

Dr. Wanda Davis

x / *the good life*

Bishop Raphael and Pastor Brenda Green
Dr. Earl Johnson
Bishop Ernestine Cleveland Reems
Bishop Harold and Pastor Brenda Ray
Bishop Walter Scott Thomas

FOREWORD

*i*this enlightening work, Dr. Lawrence Powell provides both treatise and treat to the reader, as he masterfully blends scholarly application with an experiential anecdote in his admonishment to the believer to rise above the rudimentary elements of life and grasp for the rings of the extraordinary in mind, body, and spirit.

In his polite but firm indictment of the seemingly prominent, yet entrenched preoccupation with the embrace of poverty as a guaranteed portal to heaven, Dr. Powell accurately juxtaposes the end result of such an embrace with the believer's biblical ordination to prosper and yield increase in every aspect of the his life. Indeed, as Dr. Powell makes clear, for the believer, prosperity is not merely an "option". It is a mandate! Indeed, as early as the first chapter of the Book of Genesis, the Word of God prescribes as its first command, "Be fruitful, and multiply!"

However, Dr. Powell's incitement toward "The Good Life", in contrast to the oft-assumed naked provocation toward excess, is a contrary revelation of God's providential plan and desire for every believer to prosper through recognition of, and adherence to, fundamental principles of His word and foundational protocols of His will!

It follows then, that much of this treatise is a rich assessment of barriers and hindrances to achievement of the biblically based "Good Life". Dr. Powell's acute diagnosis of barriers such as sin, unforgiveness, doubt, and other such potent deviations from the attitudinal and behavioral predicates to "good success", provides both theory and practice for the establishment of streams, if not white water rapids, of alternative sources and pathways for the fulfillment of "The Good Life".

Dr. Powell's astute recognition, and thus his fervent admonition of vocation or work as something we do as an offering to God, perhaps belies a central tenet of producing and sustaining "The Good Life". That is, "The Good Life" ultimately revolves around a fundamental investment of our capacities and opportunities as stewards of God's anointing and grace. Indeed, as Gordon Smith similarly observed in his work entitled, *Courage and Calling*:

> A vocation is sacred in that it comes from God. Whether we are called into service in the church or in the world, whether we are called to work with our hands, to religious work, to work in the arts, or to work in education and the sciences, each call has the potential for sacredness.[1]

Such prescription lies at the presumptive heart of Dr. Powell's framework of "The Good Life".

1 Smith, G. T. (2011). Courage and Calling: Embracing Your God-Given Potential. United Kingdom: InterVarsity Press, 44.

In its most revealing sense, "The Good Life", as promoted by Dr. Powell, is vested in the synergy and synchronicity of one's life choices, with the providentially scripted opportunities sovereignly granted by the will of God, who Himself declared, "For I know the thoughts that I think toward you . . . thoughts of peace and not evil, to give you a future and a hope" (Jeremiah 29:11).

The irony of that declaration is that, in and of itself, it provides the believer with the conundrum of coming to grips with the fact that, much more than we often realize, our success in life is actually less dependent upon strategizing about the future as it is upon synchronizing with our past . . . that is, the past of being succored in the spirit realm by God Himself, before being sent from eternity into time. That understanding is a key element of empowerment of our function as progressive time capsules revealing the will, purpose, and plan of God within the earth as fit vessels of transformation of life and culture.

One thing is a certainty. All who read and prayerfully digest the pages of this book will not be the same afterward. The rich and balanced presentation contained in this work will incite, excite, provoke, promote, elevate, and accelerate the believer to a whole new understanding—and hopefully, a whole new practice of living an abundant life.

Just as is the pretext of Dr. Powell's initial clarification, "The Good Life" is about much more than money. "The Good Life" is about a sense of divinely inspired and providentially directed achievement, accomplishment, and attributes that money cannot buy. It's good success. It's a quality state of being and contentment with the divine process of becoming. It's embracing and demonstrating the uncommon, the unprecedented, and the incomprehensible. It's experiencing the amazing and unveiling the unimagined.

These pages are guaranteed to provoke a robust determination to reengineer lifestyles to journey from bronze to gold. They hold the promise of life more abundantly, just as Jesus intended. Indeed, that's truly living, "The Good Life"!

—Bishop Harold Calvin Ray
Redemptive Life Fellowship, West Palm Beach, FL

INTRODUCTION

*a*h, the good life. A life of ease. A life of "No worries, mon!" A life everyone is searching for. You know it's true. You've probably imagined yourself at times dozing under that palm tree with crystal turquoise water in the background, the ocean breeze gently blowing, and the serenade of steel drums. And you look good, too, don't you?

Yes, indeed, the good life.

While this scenario sounds good (and it is), the question really is: Just what is the good life? I believe if you asked 1,000 different people this question, you would probably receive 1,000 extremely varied responses. Some would say, "it's having lots of money in the bank and no job to report to on Monday morning." Others would reply, "living in the Caribbean, napping in a hammock under a coconut tree, and sipping a drink with an umbrella in the glass." Then there are those who deem a very wealthy retirement in California, Florida, or Europe as their ultimate goal. Water-cooler talks and break rooms are filled with statements like, "I can't wait to get out of this place, get my retirement, and start living . . . (you guessed it)—the good life!"

While many equate the term "good" with their bank accounts, investments, a big house, and fancy cars, not everyone defines it that way. For example:

» Many people would consider the ability to pay their monthly bills and have food on the table the good life.
» Millions of single people flood countless numbers of online dating websites every day searching to find their perfect soulmate to secure their quest for a better life.
» Teenagers are convinced that not having to go to school and lay around the house all day would undoubtedly be an upgrade, while forty-year-olds who have found themselves without a job are enrolling in record numbers back in school to earn higher degrees.

All in search of . . . the good life!

LIFE AT THE TRUCK STOP

I once heard a story that is so indicative of today's society. While on a road trip, a family stopped at a truck stop for some fuel, drinks, and . . . well, the other reasons you usually stop! As they were about to leave, the husband was intrigued by two truck drivers who were casually standing outside enjoying their coffee, cigarettes, and solving all the world's problems. In the middle of their conversation, one of the men turned to the other and said, "Man, it's getting harder and harder to make a living out here, not to mention having any money left over." His new-found friend answered, "Well, I figure it this way: If you just lower the bar, then it's easier to live the good life." They both nodded in agreement, laughed, took another drag, and continued their conversation.

Sadly, these two truckers aren't alone. There are so many people who think the supposed "good life" is just not obtainable. They too often compare "success" to the myth of Big Foot or the Loch Ness Monster, in the fact that there just aren't enough sightings to keep them hopeful that this type of life does exist. Most journey through their whole lives trying to reach the proverbial pot of gold at the end of the rainbow, while never traveling out their front door. They are waiting for their ship to come in, but don't even know their way to the docks! In the end, their life reflects the adage, "Aim for the moon, and maybe you'll get lucky and hit a streetlamp."

And the hunt continues.

CHASING THE RAINBOW

Society's view of a better life has always been over-fantasized by the media. In the 1980s, people were enthralled by *The Lifestyles of the Rich and Famous*, which at the end of each show promised a life of "champagne wishes and caviar dreams". In the 90s, MTV's *Cribs* came rolling in, exploiting the lavishness of pop music stars, rappers, sports celebrities, and teen movie idols with a barrage of huge plasma-screen televisions, twenty-four-inch rims, and all the bling one could possibly digest. The 2000s brought us *The Real Housewives* franchise, *Filthy Rich, The Kardashians, The Rich Kids of Beverly Hills,* and on and on.

From Madonna's "Material Girl" to Bruno's "Billionaire," one thing that has become extremely evident is that the quest for a better life knows no age requirement. Teenagers today never think twice about spending hundreds of dollars for jeans full of holes, plastic shoes, a backpack adorned by a specific brand name, or a purse barely large enough to hold a tissue! All in their quest to be just like their favorite superstar.

And let's not forget the plethora of YouTubers, Instagram stars, or TikTok sensations. These platforms (and others) have taken people—young and old alike—and transformed them from job seekers to wealthy "streamers" and social media superstars. Who knew one could make millions by simply posting about their everyday life? Welcome to the twenty-first-century new wave of millionaires.

All of these pursuits come down to one thing—making money. Sadly, Christians have berated most efforts to obtain wealth for years. Why? Well, they have simply believed that having money and wealth is wrong.

Of course, the scripture used to defend these beliefs is, "Money is the root of all evil." While this would substantiate their claims, there's only one problem: This is not what the Bible says! The correct rendering of that verse is:

> "For the love of money is a root of all kinds of evil."
> —1 Timothy, 6:10

Let's break this down.

Money in and of itself is not good or evil. Neither has it ever been, nor will it ever be the single catalyst for living the good life. Far too many people live in this façade and when it's all said and done, they have merely existed—with a lot of money, yes—but yet never really lived. There is a monumental difference between the two.

Thus, the writing of this book.

A JOURNEY TOGETHER

Let me lay a little groundwork—a disclaimer of sorts—to form the onset of this book. This isn't just another book about money, a "How to Get Rich Quick!" book, or another Christian "prosperity" message. This book is not about money at all, but rather about LIFE—the good life! A few topics we will uncover are:

» What exactly IS "the good life?"
» Is it for everyone?
» Does it require certain social, economic, or *educational* standards?
» How is it obtainable?

As a believer, the good life isn't running away from you, it's running towards you!

For those who are children of the Most High God, the good life is not elusive at all. In fact, when you begin to understand what God's Word says about the life He has planned for each of His children, you'll realize you already possess everything needed to start living it right now. As a believer, the good life isn't running away from you, it's running towards you!

Arthur Ashe, one of the most successful professional tennis stars of our time, once said: "Success is a journey, not a destination. The doing is often more important than the outcome."[2] This book is about the "doing"—or the journey. It's a unique collaboration of the "super" and "natural" working together. As we begin, let's look at both of those a bit closer.

THE "SUPER"—God has set specific, irrefutable laws in place which, when adhered to and applied, will produce a higher quality of life. His divine favor is available to any believer who will dare believe it and walk therein. Once we see just how God intended us to live, our eyes and spirits are opened to pursue His provisions.

THE "NATURAL"—Whether you realize it or not, we live in a very natural world. The Bible is very specific in saying, *if we don't work, we don't eat!* (2 Thessalonians 3:10, author paraphrase) Even though we, as Christians, have a divine connection and an "inside track" to the abundant life, there will always be the elements of work ethics, budgets, and proper money management. We will explore the valuable principles in these and other areas which are directly connected to living a flourishing life.

As we begin to walk together in the following pages, I believe you will find yourself either where you have been, where you are now, or more importantly where you are heading. You will be challenged to expand your thinking, as you allow the Holy Spirit to demonstrate the truth about the abundant life that is yours through Christ.

My prayer is that as you read through these pages, you will experience the same excitement and exhilaration that grabbed

---

2   Ashe, Arthur. *Endangered Species Bulletin.* Quoted in Krishna Gifford, "Measuring Recovery Success," *US Fish & Wildlife Service*, Vol. XXXII, no. 3 (2007): 5.

hold of my spirit when God revealed these truths to me. I want you to reach further, climb higher, and desire more than what you've settled for in the past—not only in your financial life, but also in your spiritual, personal, and relational life. Most of all, I desire to raise your expectancy and challenge you to dare to believe everything that God has spoken in His Word concerning you will come to pass.

Dare to believe it and then dare to live it! I made my decision years ago that the good life is my life! Here's even better news:

The good life is your life, too!

All scripture without a notated version has been paraphrased by the author.

chapter 1

THE ORIGINAL BLUEPRINT

*f*or the majority of people, the quest to "keep up with Joneses" (whoever they are!) or have an address on "Easy Street" (wherever that is!) seems all too elusive and arduous to obtain. But it really isn't. The pattern for humankind to live abundantly and plentifully has been established for years . . . actually, since the beginning of time! And who is the grand designer of this abundant life?

God Himself!

Throughout the Scriptures—from Genesis through Revelation—God reveals His will for everyone not just to live the good life, but the BEST life ever known. It began in the Garden of Eden with its absolutely perfect living conditions. Then came Abraham, whose abundance of cattle and property made him one of the richest men to ever live up until his death (Genesis 24:1). Fast forward to King David who was one of the wealthiest men ever to live on this planet. In today's economy, King David's wealth would equate to billions of dollars! He transferred this wealth to his son, Solomon, who also became one of the wisest men ever to live. The list goes on and on. It's clear that the pattern for God to bless His people has been established throughout the ages.

Even in the New Testament.

When Jesus taught His disciples how to properly pray, He instructed them to ask for the will of God to be done on earth just like it is in heaven (Matthew 6:10). Now, I don't know if you have ever read or done any study about heaven, but by all accounts, that would be the ultimate culmination of the good life! Streets of pure gold, mansions at every address, no sickness, no poverty, no bills, no sorrow, and no end! Heaven is wonderful, but we don't have to wait until the "sweet by-and-by" to obtain the blessings of God. We can have all He has promised today in the here and now!

Let's find out how.

IT ALL STARTS WITH THE PRINTS

We are all familiar with this scenario: Robert and Kim have always dreamed of building a house from the ground up. After countless hours of driving many neighborhoods and collecting all their likes and dislikes, the time has come to put their plan into action. Their "wish list" resembles an in-depth description of a home offered by an upscale real estate firm which reads:

"Classic Mediterranean style home with cascading, spiral staircase welcoming your valued guest. This expansive estate consists of sprawling square footage and room space for a large family and guests. Oversized kitchen boasts imported countertops and marble floors. Impeccable landscaping invites you to the luscious backyard pool, spa, and outdoor entertaining area. Home encompasses three gorgeous fireplaces and is set on a large corner lot."

All the elements are ready for Robert and Kim to begin the construction of their dream home. But wait, something's missing. Just how big is that living area? How many bathrooms and where do they go? What type of lighting, tile, paint, or trees? Is the outside stucco, brick, stone, or a combination? What color are the inside walls and cabinets? Still, one of the most important questions: How can Robert and Kim ensure the architect, engineers, carpenters, painters, etc. are all on the same page? It all starts with a standardized set of plans called blueprints.

Blueprints are the benchmark for any building project, and without them, one's dreams quickly turn into nightmares!

After being involved in several construction projects, I can attest to the value of following blueprints (and the aforementioned nightmare that occurs when they're not followed). Blueprints are not only the key to a successful construction project, but they also apply in life—more specifically, in living the good life.

If God is the chief architect of the universe and our lives (which He is), then wouldn't it behoove us to know His divine blueprint for success? Absolutely, yes! The Bible says that unless the Lord builds our house, all of our labor is in vain (Psalm 127:1). Jesus es.

established one of the foundational truths that lays the groundwork to live a victorious life when He said:

> "The thief does not come except to steal, and to kill, and to destroy. I have come that they may have life, and that they may have it more abundantly." —John 10:10

Jesus came to this earth as a direct representation of God Himself (John 1:14, Hebrews 1:3a). Even though His mission was multi-faceted, one of His direct purposes was to make the abundant life available and obtainable to the entire human race. Notice, He describes this part of His assignment in two different phases: 1) that you may have life and 2) that you may have it more abundantly. It's one thing to experience life, but it's an entirely different thing to live a God-filled abundant life!

Let's take a look at these two elements.

LIFE

The word "life" in this scripture is very interesting. It's the Greek word "zoe,"[3] and it speaks of the absolute fullness of life which is in God, from God, and through God to us. In other words, we can't have the "zoe" kind of life any other way unless we receive it from God. This is also commonly referred to as "the God-kind of life". Jesus' words not only established the blueprints of how God has intended us to live but also provided the manner in which to make this abundant life accessible.

A beautiful illustration of this is found in John 11:25. Here, Jesus is standing at the tomb of his friend, Lazarus, who had died

---

3   James Strong, *Strong's Exhaustive Concordance of the Bible* (Hendrickson Publishing, 2009), s.v. "life."

four days prior. One of Lazarus's sisters, Mary, asked if her brother would live again, and Jesus answered, "I am the resurrection and the life. . . ." These, my friend, are two very distinctive traits, and here's how they both operated in this particular scenario.

A few verses later, Jesus calls Lazarus from the tomb and he immediately walked out upon His command. This was "the resurrection." But there remained a problem. Even though Lazarus was alive, he was still wrapped in his burial clothes which limited him from experiencing the fullness of life. Jesus quickly instructed the attendants to remove Lazarus's grave clothes, thus allowing him the freedom to be filled with the God-kind of life! This was "the life" in action.

It's still true today. Not only does Jesus possess the power to bring dead things back to existence, but He also carries the ability to breathe sustaining life into the things that have been resurrected!

To live the abundant life God promised, we need both!

> *Not only does Jesus possess the power to bring dead things back to existence, but He also carries the ability to breathe sustaining life into the things which have been resurrected!*

MORE ABUNDANTLY

This term in its original context means, "what is beyond; what is more than." It also represents "superabundant in quantity and superior in quality; excessive; overflowing." This is the life God desires for every believer! It's a life of excess. It's a life of more than enough. It's a life overflowing with goodness, joy, peace, health, and all manner of blessings—both spiritual and material. When you are in Christ and He is in you, God has imparted to you His superabundant, superior life. To live in and experience the very life of Almighty God is an awesome privilege . . .

. . . But it's all the more powerful to have this life—in abundance!

I'm a person who likes big things. Most of the time, I say, "The more, the better!" For example, I love seeing large families all come together for an occasion. To some, this type of gathering would seem more like organized chaos, but the energy and camaraderie of a large family are amazing to me. Abundance in other areas is great, too. Things like:

» Why settle for a few "good days" every month when you can have an abundance of joy from the Lord every day?

» While enjoying the relationship of a close friend is a good thing, branching out and experiencing the friendship of many people can provide an abundance of interaction and relationships.

» Having enough money to pay your bills is undoubtedly a blessing but think about having an abundance of money where you could substantially impact another life, family, or nation.

» What if you could trade your one day off a week for three days off without losing any pay? That would be an abundance of free time.

» To have food on the table is a blessing, but Thanksgiving usually brings an abundance of food—for the two or three days afterward, as well!

THE ORIGINAL BLUEPRINT 29

In John 6, Jesus and His disciples were on a journey when they encountered a large crowd. Hearing of their hunger and subsequent shortage of food to feed such a multitude, Jesus instructed a small boy to bring Him his lunch. After blessing it and breaking it, that small amount of food multiplied and fed over 10,000 people. That is the God-kind of life. But Jesus wasn't finished. After everyone was fed, there was enough left for that small boy and his family—plus each disciple had their own individual basket.

This, my friend, is the abundance of life!

JUST ALIVE OR REALLY LIVING?

Over the years, I have had the opportunity to associate with a diverse number of people—some very wealthy and others who live on the streets. One thing that has always caught my attention is to see the dichotomy between people's public persona and their real, private lives.

Some of the wealthiest people I have ever encountered supposedly "had it all together" outwardly, but privately, they lived in a chasm of depression and fear. They existed but were not living. On the other hand, while visiting orphanages in third-world countries, it is utterly amazing to watch children who have no monetary possessions and no connection to their families live with such joy and radiance. You can see the love for life—the "zoe" life—in their eyes; and yet measured to the world's standards, they virtually do not have any possessions.

The reason behind this is simple: Anyone living outside of God does not possess this "zoe" life. They simply breathe air and exist day-by-day, but do not live life to its fullest. I like to refer to these people as, "walking dead men". Sadly, many Christians fall into this category. While they are "in Christ," they never have the life of Christ in them! The "zoe" life is encompassed all around them, but they choose to not walk in the Truth and miss all of God's best.

It doesn't have to be this way.

The "zoe" life Jesus promised is very obtainable. God has established the blueprint and provided the means by which we can live His life on this earth. Simple enough, right? Well, then why do so many never obtain it, never live it, and never engage in this daily promise?

I'm glad you asked!

IT TAKES A THIEF

While most Christians know, at least in part, the last part of John 10:10, they neglect to read the beginning of the scripture which says:

> "The thief does not come except to steal, and to kill, and to destroy . . ."

If you can't quite comprehend this concept, allow me to make it plain: YOU HAVE AN ENEMY!

Isn't it amazing that Jesus begins this scripture with the description of your enemy—the devil? It's almost like He was saying, "Look here, there's a thief out there who has a mission to steal from you, to kill you, and eventually destroy your whole life. Now, you can let him do it, if you want; but you don't have to because I'm on a mission, as well, to give you life and a whole lot of it. And guess what? I'm stronger, more superior, mightier, and more powerful than your enemy will ever be!"

One thing about having an enemy is clear: You have a battle on your hands! In his book, *The Art of War*, ancient Chinese warrior,

Sun Tzu, taught his troops how imperative it was to know their enemy before engaging in battle. He said: "If you know your enemy and know yourself, you need not fear the results of a hundred battles. If you know yourself but not your enemy, for every victory gained you will suffer a defeat."[4]

This is true in a spiritual battle, as well.

If you're going to live the God-kind of life, here are a couple of things to know about your enemy:

Satan's ambition is your total ruin.

Your enemy's mission is to steal your money, future, dignity, joy, family, and peace. In the same manner, he's looking to kill you spiritually, ambush your dreams, and even end your life prematurely. Make no mistake about it, the "will" of the devil is your complete and total demise, and nothing less will satisfy his quest. The reason for this is quite simple: As someone made in the very image of God, you are a constant reminder of all the devil has lost and his consequent inferior position. Nothing short of your complete destruction will ever satisfy him.

Satan's nature is rooted in deception.

Contrary to popular belief, the devil is not your friend, although he may appear to be in some situations. The Bible describes him as "an angel of light," (2 Corinthians 11:14) and even goes as far as to say, "When he lies, he speaks his native language, for he is a liar and the father of all lies" (John 8:44b, NIV). I don't know anyone who has ever encountered the devil wearing a red

---

4   Sun Tzu, *The Art of War: The Oldest Military Treatise in the World*, https://www.lulu.com/shop/sun-tzu/the-art-of-war/ebook/product-1dzzwk6g.
html?q=the+art+of+war+the+oldest+military+treatise+in+the+world&page=1&pageSize=4.

suit with a pointed tail, two horns, and a pitchfork in his hand! Truthfully, he masquerades as something good, something very enticing, and clever. His appearance is rarely frightening, but predominately enticing. Satan's plans are diabolical, done in secret and in darkness.

Practically nowhere else have these characteristics been on display more than the area of money and success. For years, the Church has been deceived into many false doctrines concerning these issues. We have been hoaxed into believing such lies as: "If you have money, then there must be something wrong," or, "Holiness and poverty are synonymous." These could not be further from the truth. Yes, there are some unscrupulous rich people . . . along with some wicked poor people, too! If you don't believe me, just hang around someone who always has more month than money. They are usually more hateful than holy!

> You cannot dance with the devil and live the abundant life Jesus purchased for you.

Don't believe the lies of your enemy. If you're not careful, you'll allow him to deceive you and keep you from ever even expecting anything great. And where there is no expectancy, there will be no pursuit.

Here's something you need to never forget: You cannot dance with the devil and live the abundant life Jesus purchased for you.

Remember, Jesus called him, "The thief . . ." Now, think about it. Would you help a burglar rob your own house? Would you give him your alarm code? Would you put all your expensive things in a bag so he could find them easily? Of course not! The truth is that most of us who came upon someone illegally taking our possessions would morph into a triune superhero consisting of Rambo, The Terminator, and Jackie Chan! If we would be that serious about someone stealing our natural possessions, then how much more should we be the protectors of our spiritual lives?

There is a blueprint in the Bible for overcoming your enemy found in James 4:7:

> "Therefore submit to God. Resist the devil and he will flee from you."

One of the reasons so many Christians have fallen short of God's best is because they haven't followed one of the simplest steps of the blueprint: Instead of resisting the devil, they chose to entertain him! But the Bible is clear: If you can resist him, he will flee!

Resisting is the opposite of engaging or accepting. When your enemy comes to your door with an invitation to destruction (usually masked in something that looks good!), refuse to accept it! The quicker you resist him, the better. Playing games with the devil is only postponing the imminent outcome. Your enemy is serious about your demise; thus, you must choose to live carefully and thoughtfully—submitting to God and applying His truths to your situations and subsequent decisions.

John 10:10 very specifically describes two forces at work in your life. The good news is that one is much greater than the other. While the thief comes to destroy you, Jesus—the One who is greater than the thief, who supersedes the thief, who has defeated the thief, who is more powerful than the thief—promises the "abundant life."

It's yours for the taking!

THINK BIGGER, LIVE LARGER

To experience this God-kind of life, you most likely will have to start thinking bigger than you're thinking and living larger than you're living. You were not created to claw and scratch your way through life, live hand-to-mouth, suffer through poverty and depression, and endure illness and distress. God created you to possess power and purpose. Jesus proclaimed that through Him you can tap into this power, achieve your purpose, and begin to live the life for which God designed and destined for you.

> *God's original design for the abundant life opens the door for you to live life to the fullest.*

Deuteronomy 28:13 plainly describes God's plan: "And the Lord will make you the head and not the tail; you shall be above only, and not be beneath, if you heed the commandments of the Lord your God which I command you today, and are careful to observe them."

You can't live like the head if you're still thinking like the tail! You can't live large if you're still thinking small! You can't live abundantly if you're still thinking poverty! God's Word is jampacked full of His promises, His purpose, His power, and His prosperity. So, why in the name of good sense are so many born-again, Spirit-filled Christians still living in lack? The main reason is that they have chosen to believe their enemy—the devil—rather than follow God's divine design for life.

But that's about to change!

God's original design for the abundant life opens the door for you to live life to the fullest. He has created a wonderful world and placed you here to partner with Him, to have fellowship with Him, to be His companion, and to walk together with Him. The Bible says that the earth is the Lord's and all its fullness (Psalm 24:1). So, learn to enjoy it! Abundant living is enjoying God's creation in its fullness. Learn to live. Learn to love life. Learn to smile. Take a good vacation. (It might make you a little more pleasant and nicer to people!)

Your Heavenly Father desires for you to dare to believe His promises. Forget what you've heard in the past about the evils of money and the wickedness of wealth. Put aside the teachings that say, "Blessings are only the spiritual," "Poverty is your cross to bear," or, "Believers who desire material blessings are being carnally-minded." These mindsets and ideas are not only ludicrous—they are unscriptural!

God does not receive glory from your poverty or struggles; God receives glory from your successes and your triumphs. It's time to start living the way He designed you—according to His blueprint—and start giving God the glory He deserves!

It's time to start living *THE GOOD LIFE!*

chapter 2

THE GOSPEL OF GOOD SUCCESS

*t*here's probably no better place to start removing old mindsets than with this one: Using the words, "gospel" and "success" in the same sentence is neither doctrinal error nor blasphemous!

Even if it hasn't been verbally communicated, the unspoken ideology that has permeated the Church for decades is that if you have an abundance of money or live in a big house or drive a nice car, you must be up to something that isn't quite "kosher". Believers have bought into the "gospel of poverty" or the "gospel of just enough" for so long that when someone tries to share the message of success and blessings beyond their wildest dreams, they immediately turn a deaf ear. They equate wealth with wickedness, not realizing this type of thinking is another deceptive device of the enemy to exclude them from experiencing all of God's best. And for many, it's been too effective for too long.

Welcome to the new you!

However you have previously related money to spirituality, let this be your new mindset: You don't have to be poor to be holy, and you don't have to be evil to be rich!

You don't have to be poor to be holy, and you don't have to be evil to be rich!

I once heard a story of a family who lived in an upper, middle-class neighborhood with lovely two-story homes, swimming pools, etc. One day, they noticed a new family moving into the house one street over. As the huge moving truck was being unloaded, their attention was drawn to the driveway that was full of top-of-the-line Mercedes vehicles. They thought to themselves, *what do these people do to afford $350,000 worth of vehicles? And why are they living in our neighborhood with small children and teenagers? They must be drug dealers!*

Thinking they were doing the neighborhood a "favor," they wrote down all the license plate numbers to run a DMV background check of their own. Their unscrupulous plan would have worked perfectly, except one of the new homeowners was standing in the garage and caught them in the act! Feeling convicted to do the "neighborly thing" (which was nothing more than being nosey), they went up and introduced themselves.

THE GOSPEL OF GOOD SUCCESS 39

Without much small talk, they quickly asked, "So, what exactly do you do? What brings you here to our neighborhood?" The brief moment of silence seemed like a millennium! They were waiting for some response like, "We sell pharmaceuticals," in which case they were ready to speed dial 9-1-1, the FBI, and the DEA! The new neighbor looked at them and said, "We moved here from Miami because of ministry." They immediately responded, "Ministry? You mean like, Christian ministry?" After some dialogue, they soon became aware that one of the most recognizable names in the Latino worship world was now their new neighbor! They were relieved (to say the least) and somewhat embarrassed.

> *The issue isn't with God's desire; the problem lies with His children's unawareness of it.*

My friends aren't alone. Many Christians are programmed this way. The question is, "Why do Christians think this way?"

There is no inherent righteousness in poverty. In fact, God's Word says over and over again that His will is for His children to be blessed beyond measure, to be blessed when they rise up and when they lie down (Deuteronomy 28), to live exceedingly abundantly beyond what they can ever imagine (Ephesians 3:20), and to have dominion over the beautiful world that He created (Genesis 1:26). The issue isn't with God's desire; the problem lies with His children's unawareness of it.

GOD'S WILL

We all want to live in God's will, right? Think about how many times you've prayed, "God, show me your will. What is Your plan for my life?" In a specific sense, most people think God's ultimate desire would be for them to pray longer, fast more, commit every verse in the Bible to memory, attend church more often, give more in the offering, or witness more to others about Jesus. In and of themselves, these things are definitely important and necessary as a child of God, but according to scripture, God's greatest, first, foremost, and most significant desire is for you to be successful! If you don't believe me, just look at this scripture:

> "Beloved, I wish above all things that thou mayest prosper and be in health, even as thy soul prospereth." —3 John 2, KJV

I'm fully persuaded this passage is more than merely an apostolic greeting that addresses only "spiritual blessings". In fact, the text shows us God's heart: that blessings are to encompass our totality of being—spirit, soul, and body. Let's look at a few areas of this amazing verse in a bit more depth.

You are His Beloved.

The first word of this scripture perfectly describes God's heart toward you: "beloved." This is a tender term of endearment which means to be not just loved but "dearly loved; dear to the heart."[5] It's the same word God spoke when Jesus was baptized by John the Baptist, "This is my beloved Son, in whom I am well pleased"

---

5 Merriam-Webster Dictionary, s.v. "beloved," September, 2023, https://www.merriam-webster.com/dictionary/beloved.

(Matthew 17:5). When you think about it in this light, it's easy to see that you are just as dear to the heart of God Almighty as Jesus!

God's Top Priority.

Take particular notice of the words, "above all things." This means what is about to be said is God's top priority, first on the list, most important, el numero uno! This isn't just an after-thought. God is about to reveal His utmost intentions for you— His beloved. And what is His top desire? That you may prosper. This literally means, "to have a prosperous journey," "to lead on a good path," "to guide well," and my personal favorite, "to bring to a good conclusion."

Friend, God's not trying to ruin you. Quite the contrary. He's bringing you into prosperity. Even if life has thrown you some unexpected turns, take God at his Word. Maybe you're at a point in life where you can't even balance your checkbook and the "abundant life" Jesus promised isn't even on your radar. Don't be discouraged and make the mistake of judging your future by your current situation. Jeremiah 29:11 clearly states that God knows the plans He has concerning you, designed from the beginning of time. And what are those plans? Plans of peace and not destruc-tion, plans to prosper you and give you a future and a hope. Don't ever give up on God's promises. You're on the way to a good con-clusion if you walk in obedience to God's Word.

The Whole Package.

It's incredible how the "ultra-spiritual" contend that this verse is only referring to spiritual blessings. But you need only look at the second part to realize that God desires the whole man to experience His whole blessing.

It's evident this promise is not just addressing the spiritual aspect of prosperity. God is interested in the complete you: spirit, soul, and body. Even as your spiritual man is being developed, growing, and prospering, your physical man and soul-ish realm—your mind, will, and emotions—should also enjoy the blessings of God.

The heart of God toward His children is expressed so poignantly in this verse. Given the definitions presented, we can easily rephrase it this way:

> "Dearly beloved—the one I love as much as My Son—the foremost and dearest thing to My heart is to see you prosper. My top priority is to lead you into a prosperous journey, to walk you down a good path that concludes with success and health for your spirit, soul, and body."

This is God's ultimate desire!

TRUE DEFINITIONS

God's desire for His children has never changed, yet far too many Christians still have holy hands and empty bank accounts! Since God's will is blessings and success, it would benefit the Body of Christ to find the keys to living in His will. Let's begin with defining "The Gospel of Good Success" a bit further.

The Gospel of Good Success is:

Good News!

What a new concept for many Believers, especially those who have never experienced the abundant life! In Luke 4:18, Jesus described Himself as anointed to preach the gospel (the good news) to the poor.

The word "anointed" in this text means, "chosen by divine election."[6] Realize this: Poverty is not just a lack of money; it could be a lack of joy, peace, vision, etc. To the poor, good news is always welcome! To hear a word filled with hope and expectation can completely change someone's countenance and lift their spirits.

Some years ago, I knew a family who was so broke that the phone companies wouldn't even call them to switch! They were not only poor financially but in spirit and hope, as well. This family loved the Lord and were committed to serving God but through a series of unfortunate events, they had lost everything. One night while attending a Bible conference, this couple heard an encouraging word that breathed life into their spirits. The "good news" instantly became alive—inside them breathed a new hope—that God was with them, and it was not over! Before leaving the meeting, they placed the only dollar they had in the offering as an act of faith that God would be faithful to His Word.

Fast-forward about fifteen years. This same couple who gave their last dollar began experiencing the abundance of God beyond their imagination. And it didn't stop. Today, some twenty-five years later, their annual giving is now more than five times what their yearly income used to be! Why? Because they heard the

6   Merriam-Webster Dictionary, s.v. "anointed," September, 2023, https://www.merriam-webster.com/dictionary/anoint.

"good news," became strengthened in their spirits, and committed to being doers of the Word.

The good life isn't just for you; it's for everyone around you who needs to hear God's heart. When you begin living the "zoe" life, a lost and impoverished world will undoubtedly begin to take notice. You will become a spiritual FedEx® delivery person who has an important message for those who are not living in God's fullness:

> "You don't have to be poor anymore. You don't have to forfeit everything that belongs to you. Whatever God has spoken, it WILL come to pass when you walk in the truth, believe it, and see God's favor at work in your life!"

Believe me, "good news" works!

A "Now" Gospel

Too many Christians are convinced the abundant life Jesus speaks of in John 10:10 is only available somewhere off in the distant future in a place called Heaven. I mean, we even used to sing a hymn that said: "This world is not my home. I'm just passing through. My treasures are laid up somewhere beyond the blue."[7]

While believers do have a blessed hope of eternity, the Gospel of Good Success is a now gospel. It wasn't just for the disciples, the early Church in the Book of Acts, or for your ancestors; it's for you right now and for generations to come. The Bible says, "Today this scripture is fulfilled in your hearing" (Luke 4:21). Today, meaning, "Now, this very moment." When? NOW!

---

7   Jim Reeves, "This World is Not My Home," by J.R. Baxter, released January 28, 1962, track 11 on *We Thank Thee*, RCA Victor.

When you start walking in this revelation, your ears and eyes are opened. The Gospel of Good Success moves you from, "What am I going to do?" to, "This is the way, walk in it!" (Isaiah 30:21)

The Power of God

Romans 1:16 says the gospel—the "now" good news—is the power of God unto salvation to everyone who believes. The word "power" is translated from the Greek word "dunamis", where we derive our English word "dynamite". In reality, the gospel is an explosive power that works miracles and changes lives.

Practically every Christian will agree on the gospel's power to rescue one's soul from hell through the redemptive work of Jesus on the cross, but the very next scripture goes on to further explain how this "dunamis" power is working in our everyday lives:

> "For in it the righteousness of God is revealed from faith to faith; as it is written, 'The just shall live by faith.'" —Romans 1:17

God, in His infinite wisdom, has given you all the resources, wisdom, knowledge, and talent you will ever need to ensure your success and live a faith-filled life. Just embracing this power will cause you to begin living by faith and experiencing more and more of God's Word at work in your life.

FLIP THE SWITCH!

Walk into a dark room and what is usually the first thing you do? (This is not a trick question.) You look to turn on the lights. But why was the room dark in the first place? All the components are in place. Electrical power is running through a conduit. There's a switch on the wall and a functional light bulb screwed into the socket. But yet there was still darkness. Why? The answer is simple: Someone had to turn on the switch! There has to be a demand, a requirement, and an activation of the resident power which was ready to perform its duties. Without the simple "flip" of the switch, the room stays dark, and nothing changes.

The same concept is true concerning the power of the gospel. It has been—and forever will be—readily available. God is waiting for someone to "flip the switch" and begin walking in His divine power.

How do you flip that switch? It begins by ridding yourself of old mindsets and traditions that have held you and your loved ones back from experiencing God's best. You are not merely some "sinner saved by grace". You are His beloved, and He desires to bring you to a point of revelation that transforms your whole being from a condition of poverty to that of abundance.

Walking in this truth will open your eyes, ears, and heart. You'll begin hearing and seeing things you've never experienced. When you fully decide to get real with God—putting aside yourself, your distractions, and your religious upbringing—then you allow the power of the Holy Spirit to do the work He desires to accomplish.

This is the Gospel of Good Success: knowing God's will and walking in that revelation, being filled with His Word in your heart and mouth, and putting His Word into daily practice. This is the "good news" that our world is desperately seeking.

This is about to become your new way of life!

chapter 3

UNLOCKING THE SECRET

*S*ecrets: nuggets of truth that are kept from the masses, except for the privileged. Over the years, we have all been tantalized with the "secret of this", or the "secret of that". While the fortunate use these mysteries to accumulate great success, the general public stands hoping for the lucky day when they will learn the coveted ambiguities everyone else already knew. And then, reality kicks in . . .

. . . That day doesn't exist!

One of the top mysteries people have exploited over the last few years is their so-called "secret of success." We've all heard it; many have bought into it. But here is the real truth: Success is not a secret whatsoever! In fact, people have been enjoying it for thousands of years—long before seminars and Internet marketing campaigns.

And here's another fact you'll love knowing:

The secret to success is that there are no secrets to success!

Instead of activating some hidden code, people of great success follow principles that work unilaterally. These principles have no age, race, ethnic, or gender preferences or limitations. They just work. The key is that you just have to work them.

OUT OF THE BAG!

If you're wondering why there are no secrets to success, it's because, as my mother used to say, "Someone let the cat out of the bag!" This so-called mystery has been in print for many centuries; it's the #1 best-selling book of all time. It's not a new catchphrase, multi-level marketing program, or financial freedom webinar. No, the formula for success is found in the Old Testament of your Bible, and it reads like this:

> This Book of the Law shall not depart from your mouth, but you shall meditate in it day and night, that you may observe to do according to all that is written in it. For then you will make your way prosperous, and then you will have good success.
> —Joshua 1:8

There you go. The "secret" of good success is revealed! Let's look at a few key components of this verse to see how they apply to everyday life.

Start with the Word.

As basic as it may seem, the journey to true success begins with "The Book of the Law," which we know as the Bible. John 1:1 says, "In the beginning was the Word . . ." While we know this phrase reflects a timeframe—the genesis of everything—it can also connote the start of a particular event. For example, salvation for your soul begins by hearing God's plan of redemption.

Healing for your body starts with knowing God's promises for life and health. In the same manner, living a life of abundance commences with the Word.

Have people become wealthy without acknowledging the Word of God? Of course, they have. But you must remember that wealth does not necessarily equate to success. The question is, "Do you want to only make money, or do you want to enjoy real success?" If the latter is your goal, then you must start with the Word of God.

Talk to Yourself.

Notice where Joshua says the Word must stay . . . in your mouth! It's one thing to have the Word in your heart, but changing the way you speak is an entirely different practice. And Joshua reveals how to make that happen—by meditating.

Let's face it, the word "meditate" usually conjures images of people sitting cross-legged on the floor like a pretzel in a yoga class, intensely staring into space in a trance of deep thought. Even though that could be one way to meditate, it's not what this scripture is implying. "Meditate" in this context means "to ponder or muse; to study; to speak; to utter or mutter; to talk."[8]

---

8 Bible Study Tools, s.v. "meditate," accessed September, 2023, https://www.biblestudytools.com/lexicons/hebrew/kjv/hagah.html.

In other words, the way to keep the Word in your mouth is by talking to yourself! That's right. Speak the Word to yourself in the morning. Talk to yourself at night. Don't worry about what folks in the grocery store or at the red light think when they see you chattering and nobody's with you. You're speaking your future success into existence!

The power to make your way prosperous and secure success is found in the words which proceed out of your mouth. When you continually speak the Word of God, you are rehearsing it over and over and over. Much like a symphony orchestra, rehearsal is the key to a brilliant performance. When you rehearse speaking God's Word, then you will be ready for the real test.

> *The power to make your way prosperous and secure success is found in the words which proceed out of your mouth.*

Be a Doer

Continually speaking the Word to yourself is a great practice, but it's only half of the formula to success. You must begin doing what you've been speaking. When you do, good things are on the way! James 2:18 says it this way:

> "But someone will say, 'You have faith, and I have works.' Show me your faith without your works, and I will show you my faith by my works."

The formula is simple. If you begin with the Word, continually speak the Word, and become a doer of the Word, prosperity and good success will follow.

WALK IN STEP

Let's reveal another fact concerning success: Success does not happen by accident.

Far too many Christians believe that success and prosperity are going to fall on them like pennies from heaven. They exchange godly principles for "mailbox faith". Instead of applying the Word and cultivating good work habits, they wait on God to do some miraculous work that fills their mailbox with money and wipes out all their debt. This type of mindset has nothing to do with real faith. Real faith hears, speaks, and puts the Word into daily practice.

Success comes from a carefully planned, calculated life. Best-selling author and one of the world's best communicators on motivation, Zig Ziglar, once said: "You were born to win, but to be a winner you must plan to win, prepare to win, and expect to win!"[9]

Plan. Prepare. Expect.

Have you ever seen a mouse running through a maze to get a piece of cheese? It's one of the most fascinating things to watch. That little guy runs and runs, hitting walls and finding different paths until he finally discovers the right way. And then, "Bingo!" He finds the cheese! This activity is cute for a mouse, but painstakingly sad for humans. Yet, many people—Christians

---

9   Zig Ziglar and Tom Ziglar, *Born to Win: Find Your Success*, read by Andy Andrews. Made for Success, 2017. Audiobook.

included—live their entire lives in this exact same manner, all in search of the "cheese" at the end of the road.

Friend, living the good life does not happen this way! The path, preparation, and process of success are exact. Consider this scripture:

> "The steps of a good man are ordered by the Lord, and He delights in his way." —Psalm 37:23

The word "steps" infers activity and movement. You can't be walking with God and constantly sitting on the couch of life at the same time! But when God orders your steps, it means you're walking in cadence with Him—thoughtfully, with purpose, and with progression. There's nothing haphazard about that journey. When God gives the marching orders, you immediately move—in time and in step with His directives and plans.

The Bible says that God will never leave you nor forsake you! (Hebrews 13:5b) When God is ordering your steps, you're not left to your own devices to struggle through the maze of life in hopes of maybe coming to a good conclusion. God is with you every step of the way. When you walk in this way, unparalleled success awaits you, and the Creator of the universe delights in your way!

Many people think God is never pleased with them; but according to this scripture, when you follow God, it brings Him great joy and delight. You can have all the money in the world, but if God is displeased with your life, at the end of the day, you've failed miserably. This is what the Bible calls "true riches," which we will examine in a later chapter.

THE PROMISE

Let's jump back to Joshua 1:8 for a moment. That promise from God is so simple, yet many times Christians feel the need to complicate things for validation. In their religious mind, it would make more sense if God said, "Meditate on the Word day and night, go to church three times a week, serve on two committees, pray an hour in the morning and an hour in the evening, and fast two days a week. For then, you will make your way prosperous, and then you will have good success." Thank God those are not the requirements! However, while the process of success is not complicated, it is exact and precise.

Know the Word. Speak the Word. Do the Word.

Years ago, I heard an old-time preacher say something I've never forgotten and have put into practice over the years. He said: "If you put the Word of God in you when you don't need it, it will be there when you do need it!" I can attest to the power and truth of that statement.

> *Know the Word. Speak the Word. Do the Word.*

Your enemy will do everything in his power to stop you from living the abundant life God has promised. When he comes and tries to discourage you, just open up your mouth and do what you've been doing all day—speak the Word.

When you're attacked with thoughts of lack and failure, say, "It is written, 'My God shall supply all my needs according to His riches in glory by Christ Jesus'" (Philippians 4:19, author paraphrase).

When your enemy launches an arsenal against your family, say, "It is written, 'All my children shall be taught by the Lord, and great shall be the peace of my children'" (Isaiah 54:13, author paraphrase).

If you feel alone and unwanted, say, "It is written, 'For He Himself has said, "I will never leave you nor forsake you!"'" (Hebrews 13:5, author paraphrase).

That Bible sitting on your nightstand, stashed away on your bookshelf, or hidden deep in your cell phone apps contains a veritable arsenal. Pick it up! Read it! Meditate on it! Speak it! There is a promise waiting for you when you do.

That promise, according to Scripture, is prosperity and good success. We know these are gifts from God, but I want to bring your attention to how they come to fruition in your life:

> "For then YOU will make your way prosperous, and then YOU will have good success." —Joshua 1:8b

Did you see that? Scripture plainly says that all of your success in life is coming through you! That's right—you, not God.

Who's going to make your way prosperous? YOU ARE. Who's going to bring you good success? YOU ARE. Your success isn't up to God—it comes through you! Everyone has the same promise, yet not everyone enjoys the same benefits. Why? Because God's promise of prosperity and success only comes to those who follow the "secret":

» Know the Word.
» Speak the Word.
» Do the Word.
» Walk in step with God.

The Word of God is light. It's living. It's Spirit. It's creative. By speaking the Word that is overflowing from your believing heart, you release the anointing of God on your life. That anointing carries miracles, healing, prosperity, peace, joy, etc. Open your mouth and speak what God says about your situation. Stop speaking failure and begin speaking success. When you do, just watch how your life will begin to immediately change once you hear, meditate, speak, and do the Word. It's a process with promise.

This, beloved, is the true "secret to success" that's not a secret any longer!

chapter 4

SUCCESS: WHAT IT IS AND HOW TO OBTAIN IT

*i*n our last chapter, we briefly touched on the subject of real success. However, defining "success" would be just as varied as describing "the good life". Everyone has their own interpretation of what it means to be "successful". In this chapter, we're going to dive into two elements of success: 1) what it is, and 2) how to obtain it.

DEFINING SUCCESS

For far too long, scores of people have concluded that success is equated only to having money. Their philosophy is, "The more money you have, the more successful you are." It's the world's way of establishing a standard of living—or better yet, a standard of "successful living". However, this is a false hypothesis of true success.

The question that faces many Christians has always been, "Is it God's desire for me to have money?" The answer is emphatically, "Yes!" but not at the expense of your emotional health and spiritual development. You see, too many people live for the almighty dollar instead of living for the Almighty King, allowing Him to bring sufficiency to their lives.

God desires for you to have true success, which is far more than having money in the bank. What good is it to have tremendous wealth yet live a life full of stress, depression, loneliness, and fear? That's not the abundant life Jesus came to give us. On the other hand, it's entirely possible to have a bank account full of money and a heart full of peace, joy, and love. In fact, this is the whole-being success and prosperity God intends for you.

SUCCESS FROM GOD'S PERSPECTIVE

To understand the true meaning of anything in life, you must first seek what God says about the matter. This same principle applies to being successful. What does God say about it? The answer is quite simple: To be truly successful, you must fulfill the purpose for which you were created.

> . . . To be truly successful, you must fulfill the purpose for which you were created.

God has a divine purpose for everyone on this earth. He did not put you on this planet without any forethought. Remember Jeremiah 29:11, which says, "For I know the plans I have for you" (NIV).

This scripture tells us that 1) God is a planner, and 2) He has plans—specific strategies and divine purposes—for your life.

True success, in God's eyes, is not measured by your possessions, popularity, performance, or prestige. These might grant you some temporary accomplishments and even some material gain, but in the end, if you have not fulfilled your reason for existence, then true success has not been obtained.

For instance, if God called you to the medical field, but you're driving a truck, you can be the wealthiest truck driver with the biggest, most chrome-covered rig on the super highway, and not be experiencing real success. Likewise, if God called you to drive trucks and you walk around in green scrubs with a stethoscope around your neck all day, you're not truly successful—no matter how much money you make. Why? Because true success is defined by progressively moving toward God's purpose for your life.

> *. . . true success is defined by progressively moving toward God's purpose for your life.*

Some people look at pastors who have 10,000 members and think, Wow, he's successful! But what if God has called him to the business world and not the ministry? No matter how many members he attracts, his purpose in life would be eluding him and he would not have true success. In God's eyes, success comes down to three things:

» Becoming who God designed you to be.
» Doing what God created you to do.
» Possessing what God wants you to own.

SUCCESS AND MONEY

Even though success cannot be measured solely by monetary gain, money is a component. As President Ronald Regan once said, "Money can't buy happiness, but it certainly can provide a better class of memories."[10] Having money is not wrong; however, material possessions gained outside of God's perspective and plan for your life will often produce more frustration than accomplishments, more anger than triumph, and more greed than financial increase.

Jesus taught His disciples this principle when He said, "For what profit is it to a man if he gains the whole world, and loses his own soul?" (Matthew 16:26) The businessman with a huge salary, a Rolls Royce, and a private jet is rich, but is he successful? According to the Bible, if he doesn't have a relationship with God through His Son, Jesus, then he is not. Understand this: Material abundance is not the mark of true success, but rather a byproduct of successful living.

> *Material abundance is not the mark of true success, but rather a by-product of successful living.*

10 Ronald Reagan, "Money can't buy happiness, but it certainly can provide a better class of memories," AZ Quotes, Sept. 2023, https://www.azquotes.com/quote/527433.

A few years ago, MasterCard® filled the airwaves with commercials reminding us that everything in life doesn't carry a price tag. Scenes of a father and son at a baseball game flash images of tickets, $45; hot dogs and drinks, $18; souvenir baseball cap, $20; uninterrupted time with a ten-year-old, priceless! The message is true; there are things in life—a life full of peace, joy, and health—no amount of money can buy.

SUCCESS IS A GOAL

Take a look at how Webster's Dictionary defines success: "The degree or measure of succeeding; a favorable outcome or result; the attainment of wealth, favor, or eminence."[11] The word "succeed," from which we get the word "success," means "to attain a desired object or end."[12] In other words, one way to measure success is by reaching a desired goal.

Take weight loss, as an example. Let's say you have a goal to lose fifty pounds before your upcoming twenty-year class reunion. You know some old girlfriends or boyfriends will be there, and you don't want to walk in carrying around that spare tire or those saddlebags you've acquired in the past twenty years! Salads now take the place of burger value meals, and the treadmill replaces your favorite television shows. The class reunion comes around and you've lost thirty pounds. Have you been successful? In the truest sense of the word, no. Sure, you lost some weight and surely look and feel better, but you fell short of your desired goal.

---

11 Merriam-Webster Dictionary, s.v. "success," September, 2023, http://www.merriam-webster.com/dictionary/success.
12 Merriam-Webster Dictionary, s.v. "succeed," September, 2023, http://www.merriam-webster.com/dictionary/succeed.

You're definitely on the way, but success lies in dropping the remaining twenty pounds.

Now that we have established some guidelines on what true success is, the question then arises, "How do you become successful?" Here are some key factors to help lead you into your new life of success.

OBTAINING SUCCESS

In our last chapter, we examined some principles from Joshua 1:8, primarily the value of continually speaking God's Word. When you do this, the Bible promises "good success". According to Strong's Bible Dictionary, the word "success" in this scripture carries several meanings such as: "being circumspect; intelligent; prudent; wisely understanding with insight and comprehension." By these definitions, it's plain to see that true success is inherently and inextricably linked to the wisdom of God.

King Solomon, a prime example of wealth and wisdom, reiterates this point in two of his writings:

". . . But wisdom brings success" (Ecclesiastes 10:10b)

"Wisdom is the principal thing; Therefore get wisdom. And in all your getting, get understanding" (Proverbs 4:7).

. . . True success is inherently and inextricably linked to the wisdom of God.

How did Solomon become so rich and enjoy much success? Simple. He asked for and received the wisdom of God. It's still the foundational key to success today. A life built on the wisdom of God produces many benefits, some which are:

Stability (Isaiah 33:6)

Truly successful people—especially those who experience it for the long-haul—build their lives around stability. That's not to say they don't take risks or live boring lives. Quite the contrary. When your life is grounded in the wisdom of God, the world around you could be completely caving in, but you stand strong in the midst of chaos.

Value and Admiration (Proverbs 3:35)

Each year, individuals are awarded the Pulitzer and Nobel Peace Prize for their outstanding, recognizable work in literature or public service. In the same manner, celebrities and athletes alike are continually admiring their parents, coaches, and mentors for their "words of wisdom". Whether you are winning international recognition or respect from your peers, wisdom is the door to admiration.

Favor in High Places (Proverbs 14:35)

Have you ever noticed how some people, even though not the most naturally qualified, seem to receive promotions and blessings? Maybe they lacked the proper education or experience, but still are highly successful. This, my friend, is a result of hard work and favor—and favor comes to those who operate in divine wisdom. One thing I have learned is you cannot reach success and enjoy the good life on your own. People will have to show you favor, and wisdom is the "favor magnet"!

Riches (Proverbs 14:24)

King Solomon easily proves this point. The wisest man who ever lived was one of the richest men who ever lived. Pretty simple!

Long Life (Proverbs 4:10)

The Bible promises long life to those who walk in wisdom and do not live in the way of the wicked. Not only can wise habits add years to your physical life, financial wisdom can multiply your assets and extend your legacy. Whatever wisdom touches lives long.

Safety and Security (Proverbs 2:11-12)

The storms of life are inevitable and show no favoritism. Jesus said that the wise man (he who listens to His words and does them) builds his house on the rock, while foolish men build on sand (Matthew 7:24-26, author paraphrase). Wisdom is the primary element to your safety and security, no matter what life may throw your way.

ADDING THE NATURAL

Learning and walking in the wisdom of God is the primary step to success, but it's not the end all be all. Along with spiritual wisdom, you must also obtain the natural education and training required to accomplish your set goals. And take it from me, it's never too late! (I earned my doctorate at age fifty-two!)

A lady in our church came up to me one day and said that she had just enrolled in college to study interior design. This had been a dream of hers for years. I rejoiced with her decision and then asked her, "Ma'am, if you don't mind me asking, how old are you?" She replied, "I'm sixty years old!" It is never too late to gain the intelligence and education you need for a successful journey. Benjamin Franklin invented bifocals at age seventy-six. Colonel Sanders was sixty-five when he launched Kentucky Fried Chicken®. Start now investing in your education. Elevate your understanding and knowledge and watch God work on your behalf.

Even if you consider yourself naïve and uneducated, God's Word promises to give you understanding (Psalm 119:130). Don't be discouraged, regretting your lack of education or lack of book knowledge. God promises that His wisdom is available to all His children.

THE INGREDIENT OF FAITH

Spiritual and natural wisdom are two foundational building blocks for success, but to fully activate all the promises of God in your life, there's another piece to the puzzle: faith.

No matter how much you know or how much you obtain, you will never achieve an overflowing life without faith in the One who created you and sees you through to the end, in His power. To obtain true success, your life must be pleasing to Him, and the Bible says it is impossible to please God without faith (Hebrews 11:6).

What exactly is faith? Hebrews 11:1 describes it as:

> ". . . the substance of things hoped for, the evidence of things not seen."

Faith is substance—not a strong emotion, a steadfast conviction, or a determined will. Faith isn't something you manufacture on your own, but rather it's a gift from God (Ephesians 2:8) that comes from hearing His Word (Romans 10:17). To hear something once usually isn't enough to remember it, let alone re-speak it. Faith comes from a constant, continuous flow of hearing—much like the waters of a mighty river whose flow cannot be contained.

One of the best ways to hear the Word is for it to flow out of your mouth. Think about it. There's only one person (outside of God) who's with you 24/7. That person is you! Since you are with you all the time, speak the Word to yourself and build your faith. You can speak and hear the Word anytime, anywhere—in the bedroom, in the bathroom, and in the boardroom. Even when you find yourself in a situation where you can't speak out loud, speak the Word silently to yourself in your heart. The more you hear it, the more faith is released—and the more pleasing you become to God.

Now, you are positioned for great success and great blessing!

A SUDDEN BURST

If you're one who believes the term "non-profit organization" is not a doctrinal stance embraced by God but instead a legal classification for religious entities, then it's time to clean out what's been lodged in between your temples. It's time to experience God's best!

Look at the pattern we have already seen. First, God says that His ultimate will for you is that you prosper—spirit, soul, and body. Then He gives you the formula for success. And if that wasn't enough, now He's teaching you how to profit:

"Thus says the Lord, your Redeemer, the Holy One of Israel: 'I am the Lord your God, who teaches you to profit, who leads you by the way you should go." —Isaiah 48:17

I love to break down this verse.

The word "profit" means "to derive benefit."[13] "Benefit" is a combination of two words: "bene" meaning "good,"[14] and "fit" meaning "a sudden burst or flurry of activity."[15] These definitions bring a scenario to mind that we've all experienced too many times.

Have you ever seen a child throw a fit right in the middle of a store or restaurant? You would definitely categorize that as a sudden burst of activity, right? Well, put this example together with the Isaiah 48:17 scripture, and here's what you see: When God teaches you to profit, He pours a sudden burst of blessings into your life!

One of the most awe-inspiring sights in the world is Niagara Falls. The sheer power and majesty of six million cubic feet of water falling over the crest line every minute is unfathomable. The water is so forceful that you can hear the sound from nearly a mile away. Not only is it a beautiful sight to behold, but what a remarkable example of God rushing blessings upon you. Now, would you rather be under the drip of a spout or the rush of Niagara Falls? I believe the answer is pretty obvious! Why settle for a drip here and a drip there, when God is pouring out a sudden burst of blessings?

Those blessings are for you!

13 Merriam-Webster Dictionary, s.v. "profit," September, 2023, https://www.merriam-webster.com/dictionary/profit.
14 Online Etymology Dictionary, s.v. "benefit," accessed September, 2023, https://www.etymonline.com/search?q=benefit.
15 Online Etymology Dictionary, s.v. "fit," accessed September, 2023, https://www.etymonline.com/all/fit.

GET STARTED

In this chapter, we have examined the true meaning of success and how to obtain it. Now, let's start living the good life! Are you ready? If so, here are a few simple steps to jumpstart your journey into motion.

Leave Where You Are

There comes a point in everyone's life where "enough is enough!" Until you get sick and tired of where you are, you're never going to journey into what God has for you. You can't live in the Promised Land and Egypt at the same time! You must leave where you are and whole-heartedly possess what God has promised.

See the Big Picture

Imagine for a moment the large canvas on which God designed your life. No matter what it looks like all around you right now, know that God is painting a picture of prosperity, abundance, and blessing beyond measure! The Bible says that God's ways are higher than your ways and His thoughts are higher than your thoughts (Isaiah 55:9). See what God sees; think what God thinks; and pursue His ways.

Move Forward

If you feel as though your past life, race, education, gender, or age has disqualified you from living the abundant life, let me set the record straight: That's a lie straight from the pit of hell! And why wouldn't your enemy lie? That's his nature, remember? It's time to no longer be paralyzed by the tragedies that have happened in your life. It's time to move forward into the promises of God.

Have you ever noticed how small your car's rearview mirror is compared to the windshield? The reason is simple: It's more important to see what's ahead of you than what's behind you. The same holds true in your journey of success. Don't focus on the past. You can't change it. Learn from it and move forward. When your faith and trust is in Jesus Christ, your past is history, and your future success is God's desire.

Dare to Believe

Success is not some "pie in the sky" fairy tale only reserved for those who have the right last name or have stumbled upon good fortune. The good life is available for anyone who will believe and activate faith. Wherever you are in life right now, do something that will make you reach further, climb higher, and desire more than what you've settled for in the past. I'm not talking about material gain only. Desire more in your spiritual life, your personal life, your family life, and your financial life.

Believe the good life is for you, then go for it! Start every day by asking yourself, "What would I attempt today if I knew I could not fail?" Then dare to believe it . . . and then dare to live it! Remember, you were born to succeed, not to fail.

Go! Be what you were born to be!

GOOD

LIFE

chapter 5

EIGHT ENEMIES OF SUCCESS

*n*ow that we've determined the meaning of "true success", and seen clear steps of how it's obtainable, the question remains, "Why doesn't everybody live this life?" Like anything else in life, if it were easy, everyone would be living it! But remember the scripture we saw in chapter one? It very clearly states that just as God has provided a way for you to live the abundant life, there is also an enemy that has employed very strategic devices in which to steal your God-ordained life of success. Let's unveil eight of the most common enemy tactics that can keep you from living an abundant, successful life.

ENEMY #1: SIN

As unpopular as this subject is in today's religious society, it does not negate the fact that sin is still one of the primary enemies of success. Now, when most people hear the word "sin", they immediately begin to imagine a list of evil activities such as fornication, lying, stealing, adultery, etc. Even though these are sinful activities, the Bible gives a much more, all-encompassing description of sin. Romans 14:23 says: "Whatever is not from faith is sin." First John 5:17 puts it this way: "All unrighteousness is sin."

What most Christians don't realize is that anytime you fail to believe God and walk in unbelief, it's sin. Let's take that a step further. What about when you refuse to believe God's Word concerning prosperity and success? Or when you fail to believe you're forgiven and that you can do all things through Christ? Believing anything contrary to the Word of God—no matter the subject—is sin.

If there's one thing I have learned about the devil over the years, it's that even though he's evil, he's not stupid! If he can get you to doubt what God's Word says about you, and subsequently cause you to walk in doubt, fear, anxiety, and worry, then he's winning.

Solomon knew a thing or two about the relationship between sin and success. He writes:

> "He who covers his sins will not prosper." —Proverbs 28:13

Some scriptures need elaboration, but not this one. It's plain and simple: When you try to whitewash your sin, you will not succeed. In today's permissive standards, it's easy to allow the popular, laissez-faire attitude to invade your life. But it's a trap. Don't fool yourself into thinking you can come to church on Sunday and pretend to have complete devotion to God, and then live like the devil Monday through Saturday and expect God to bless your life.

It just doesn't work.

How do you know you're living in sin? There are many markers, but one that stands out is disobedience. The Bible clearly states that obedience brings blessings and success, and disobedience brings failure (Deuteronomy 28). Clearly, the cost of disobedience is serious, but the blessings of obeying God's voice are countless!

> *When you try to whitewash your sin, you will not succeed.*

ENEMY #2: LOOSE LIPS

You can always identify one's position in life by what comes out of their mouths. Just hang around someone for a few minutes, and you'll know! Think about the people you greet with a simple question like, "How are you doing?" and their answer is a deluge of frustrations and dilemmas. It won't be long before you start to avoid those people because you know what to expect.

Contrary to popular belief, talk is not cheap. Actually, the words that come out of your mouth can cost you more than you can imagine. Matthew 12:37 is a Kingdom principle which says:

> "For by your words you will be justified, and by your words you will be condemned."

Just how powerful are your words? According to this Scripture, what you say either leads to your salvation or declares you guilty.

Psalm 45:1 says that your tongue is the pen of a writer. Every day, ask yourself, "What am I writing about my life today? What am I writing about other people?" To enjoy God's success in life requires your words not to produce condemnation, but rather righteousness and life.

Do you remember the school-age adage that said, "Sticks and stones may break my bones, but words will never hurt me?" That's ridiculous! I'm convinced the person who came up with that ludicrous philosophy—even though it was meant to be some form of encouragement and consolation—didn't know what the Bible says about the power of words. Lips that speak foolish words lead to all sorts of contention, adversity, and eventual ruin. The Bible is full of principles concerning the power of words. For example:

> "A fool's lips enter into contention, and his mouth calls for blows. A fool's mouth is his destruction, and his lips are the snare of his soul. . . . Death and life are in the power of the tongue . . ." (Proverbs 18:6-7, 21). Psalm 34:12-13 says, "Who is the man who desires life and loves many days, that he may see good? Keep your tongue from evil and your lips from speaking deceit." Finally, Proverbs 6:2 declares: "You are snared by the words of your mouth."

The words that proceed out of your mouth chart your course of success or defeat. To control your mouth is to control your future. It's not only paramount to your success but is also a necessity to your witness for Christ. No one who has blessings and cursing coming out of their mouths at the same time can truly glorify God. Begin to paint the picture of your life with the words you speak, and watch God begin to honor His Word—the Word that's coming out of your own mouth!

To control your mouth is to control your future.

ENEMY #3: BROKEN PROMISES

Of all the enemies listed in this chapter (and they are not an exhaustive list), nothing can ruin your reputation and derail your progress any quicker than broken promises. People make commitments and then struggle to fulfill them. For example, the promise to "love, honor, and cherish, till death do you part" is broken in divorce courts every day. People borrow money, and instead of paying it back, they go on vacation to Hawaii and send their lender a "Wish you were here!" postcard! (One day, the lender is going to send a postcard back that says, "Great! I'll be there in a few hours to collect my money!")

While I love the age of evolving technology, at times I do long for the simplicity of truth found in yesteryears. Before the days of contracts, corporate attorneys, loan papers, credit checks, and non-compete agreements, there was a saying that "A man's word was his bond." What this simply means is someone's word was good enough. Their integrity was on the line; thus, it provided enough motivation to make sure whatever was agreed upon would come to pass.

Anyone who has been in business for any length of time will tell you that no one can succeed or have any longevity of success with a reputation for breaking promises. If being in business for yourself is God's plan for your life, let me give you a quick word of advice: You cannot make it a practice to take advantage of people and expect growth.

> *You cannot make it a practice to take advantage of people and expect growth.*

Unfortunately, broken promises are not just limited to unbelievers! People now know they need to watch out for the ones who profess to be Christians, as well. I heard a man comment, "You better watch those people who have a fish on their business card. It usually means they are going to take you hook, line, and sinker." How sad that one of the universal symbols of Christianity has now become a warning sign in the business community. Even more tragic are the unsaved spouses and employees who can't understand how one can be praising God on Sunday but not honor their word throughout the week. The bottom line is you must be a person of truth if success is going to inhabit your home or business.

Over the years, I've witnessed people from all walks of life constantly struggle with this issue. Most of them really want to change, but years of behavioral patterns are sometimes hard to break. If this is you, let me encourage you to start being a person of your word—even in seemingly insignificant things. Here are a few items to help get you started.

» Be careful to commit to only those things which you can fulfill.
» Set a goal to be early for every appointment and engagement.
» Remember this acronym: UPOD. "Under Promise, Over Deliver." Exceed expectations.
» Set small promises, like having ice cream with your child or attending a school function, and keep it. Be on time!

Remember, your reputation is at stake with every commitment, every contract, every loan, and every promise. Let your word be your bond and watch God promote you to success.

ENEMY #4: UNFORGIVENESS

The issue of unforgiveness is rampant in our society and crippling to the forward progression of any life. For any Christian, forgiveness is not a suggestion; it is required by God.

Jesus painted a marvelous picture of true forgiveness to His disciples in the parable found in Matthew 18:23-35. Here, Jesus tells of a king who had many servants, who owed him money, one an extremely excessive amount. When the king decided to collect the debts, the servant with the most massive deficit begged for forgiveness. The king found compassion in his heart, consequently forgiving his large mass of accumulated debt.

Immediately, the servant who was forgiven the equivalent of millions of dollars found a man who owed him about $10. When the amount could not be paid, the forgiven servant demanded this man be thrown in jail—over ten bucks! When the news of this unmerciful act reached the king, he promptly responded: "You wicked servant! I forgave you all that debt because you begged me. Should you not also have had compassion on your fellow servant, just as I had pity on you?' And his master was angry, and delivered him to the torturers until he should pay all that was due to him."

Jesus ended this parable with the Kingdom principle of:

"So My heavenly Father also will do to you if each of you, from his heart, does not forgive his brother his trespasses."
—Matthew 18:35

One of the ways unforgiveness keeps you from the good life is by hindering your prayers. Undoubtedly, answered prayer is a key ingredient to a happy, successful life. Jesus addressed this very issue in Mark 11:25-26. Make no mistake, you can pray all day long for good health, prosperity, peace, joy, and the favor and blessings of God, but if you are harboring unforgiveness, your prayers have a ceiling and will not be effective.

The seed of unforgiveness will keep you entangled in your past and never allow you to progressively pursue your future. You must let it go. Yes, this may be very difficult—maybe seemingly impossible. But instead of focusing on what was done to you, consider what unforgiveness can cost you. This could be the motivation you need to forgive . . . and forgive often.

I love how renowned Christian author, Lewis B. Smedes, describes the power of unforgiveness: "To forgive is to set a prisoner free and discover that the prisoner was you."[16] Friend, it's time to be free and live the amazing life God has planned for you.

> *The issue of unforgiveness is rampant in our society and crippling to the forward progression of any life.*

ENEMY #5: UNFAITHFUL STEWARDSHIP

Here's a little wake-up call: Everything you claim to possess isn't yours! That's right. Everything you have is on loan to you from God. The Bible says that the earth is His and everything that dwells in it (Psalm 24:1, author paraphrase). The house you own, the car you drive, the children you raise, the gold on your finger and around your neck, the money in your bank account, your time and talents—it all belongs to God. And don't think for one second that you can just do whatever you want to with it all. No, God not only expects but commands you to be faithful with everything He's given you.

From Adam and Eve in the Garden until today, God has always required His people to be faithful stewards of His blessings. The word "stewardship" means, "the careful and responsible management of something entrusted to one's care."[17] This simply means that whatever God has entrusted to your safekeeping

---

16 Lewis B. Smedes, *Days of Grace Through the Year* (InterVarsity Press, 2007), p. 242.
17 Merriam-Webster Dictionary, s.v. "stewardship," September, 2023, https://www.merriam-webster.com/dictionary/stewardship.

or put under your authority, you are responsible to use for His glory and His honor.

It never ceases to amaze me how many people look all around them to try and find that "magic" thing that will catapult them into success. They go here, run over there, sign up for this webinar, attend that meeting, try to befriend someone who they think can help them, etc. All the while, everything they need to live the best life they could ever imagine isn't around them, it's on the inside of them! Here's the missing link: Those God-given talents and abilities won't produce a single thing unless they are properly developed and managed.

This is true for you, too!

If you think God gifted you with incredible talents just so you can sit around and waste them, think again! In Luke 19:13, Jesus told His disciples to, "Do business till I come." This means to be busy, to make something happen, to get involved in Kingdom work—financially, spiritually, emotionally, vocationally, and relationally. Those deposits on the inside of you are there for you to work, and then be smart with the increase God provides.

There's nothing wrong with believing God to make you a millionaire. (It won't magically fall out of the sky!) But instead of looking at the million, how about starting by adequately managing the $50,000 a year you make now? Do you faithfully tithe and give offerings to God? Do you have a savings program or any investment strategy? Do you live on a budget and believe God for increase? In other words, are you a good steward of what God has already given you?

Start where you are. To live an abundant, overflowing life, you first must be found faithful with the resources entrusted to you. When you are found faithful in the small things, you will become ruler over much (Luke 16:10, author paraphrase). Stewardship is a significant key to blessing and increase. Without it, you'll be like that mouse in the maze—always running and running but never succeeding.

ENEMY #6: DOUBLE-MINDEDNESS

There are no boundaries on where you can find people who are double-minded! They are everywhere—in the business world, church, classroom, marriage relationships, etc. If you have ever dealt with someone who falls into this category or perhaps have had to overcome this trait in your own life, you understand why it's an enemy of success. It's extremely difficult for people who are continually changing directions or allegiances to enjoy the good life.

The Bible says a lot about this subject and the dangers it holds. The Book of James likens double-mindedness to instability, describing that person as one tossed by the wind, never receiving anything from the Lord (James 1:6-8, author paraphrase). To be double-minded also means to be double-spirited. Think about that for a minute. When someone is double-spirited, it means they have two spirits competing for their allegiance. Physics confirms that two objects can't inhabit the same space at the same time. What this means in the spiritual realm is that doubt and faith cannot occupy your mind concurrently. Jesus said it this way:

> ". . . Have faith in God. For assuredly, I say to you, whoever says to this mountain, 'Be removed and be cast into the sea,' and does not doubt in his heart, but believes that those things he says will be done, he will have whatever he says."
> —Mark 11:22b-23

When you believe, you receive; when you doubt, you go without. No wonder your enemy uses the weapon of double-mindedness so frequently! If he can get you to doubt that the good life even exists, then he's won the battle.

Living in God's best requires single-mindedness, commitment, and stability. Those who rise above their emotions and believe the Word, regardless of the circumstances that surround them, will eventually walk in the fullness God has planned for their lives. To live this life, you have to decide, once and for all, to believe God and reject every idea that is contrary to His Word. It all goes back to knowing God's Word, speaking God's Word, and doing God's Word.

> *When you believe, you receive; when you doubt, you go without.*

ENEMY #7: BAD COMPANY

When I was growing up, my mother and father were very guarded concerning my friends. When I wanted to go to someone's house to play, the detailed information my parents required read like a job application to the Secret Service! Not only did they have to know the kid, but also their parents, address, phone number, next of kin, blood type, who else was going to be there, and what we were planning on doing (hour-by-hour)! I probably didn't agree with their methodology at the moment, but now having raised three children of my own, I don't think they were strict enough!

In every part of life—whether raising kids or building a business—the company you keep can determine your success or failure. A very powerful scripture concerning this issue is found in 1 Corinthians 15:33, where Paul writes:

> "Do not be deceived: 'Evil company corrupts good habits.'"

Falling in with the wrong crowd can be detrimental, even costing you your divine destiny. I'm not just talking about unethical or unscrupulous relationships, but also the ones close to you who are a constant drain of energy, creativity, and positive motivation. Those types of relationships are called leeches. Take my word for it; when you begin to experience success in any area of life, they will hunt you down until they latch on!

Here's a good exercise. Stop right now and take inventory of the people closest to you. Are they always talking you down? Do they always see the glass as "half-empty"? Do they live in constant fear of the future? These are leeches, and as harsh as it might sound, they have to go for you to move on with what God has in store for your life!

The life of Jesus is an excellent example of keeping the right company. During His earthly ministry, Jesus spent time with three types of people: 1) those He ministered to, 2) those who received His ministry, and 3) those who ministered to Him. We never see in the scriptures where Jesus kept close association with His critics. As a matter of fact, His instructions to the disciples, when they encountered someone who would not receive them or their message, was to ". . . shake off the dust from your feet" (Matthew 10:14).

That same principle is true, today!

If you're going to experience all that God has in store for you, you have to learn to go where you're celebrated, not just tolerated! Find your "good company" who believes in you, encourages you, rejoices with you, and even loves you enough to say what you need to hear, not just what you want to hear on occasion. The Bible says that if you walk with the wise, you too will be wise (Proverbs 13:20, author paraphrase). Search out these types of relationships. They can catapult you to greatness, quickly!

ENEMY #8: RESISTANCE TO CHANGE

There's an old saying which says, "The only people who like change are babies in dirty diapers!" The older you live, the more you see just how true this is! In over thirty years of pastoring, I have found that people, in general, do not like change. But the truth is, one of the only constants in life—besides God—is change! Those who live successful lives not only embrace change, but they welcome the challenges it brings and position themselves to benefit from them.

On many occasions, change is a good thing and a necessary component of success. Change means newness, regeneration, and growth. Nowhere is this more evident than in the world of technology. Today, cell phones contain more computing power than what was used to put a man on the moon in the 1960s! Home goods, entertainment, and even groceries are now ordered at the click of a button and ready for pick up or delivery within a few hours. Jeff Bezos, founder/CEO of Amazon® and 2020's richest man in the world, is a classic example that those who embrace and are proponents of change not only survive but thrive in their field of expertise.

One way to help ensure that your future looks better than your past is to do something different in the present. Don't make the mistake of waiting until "something happens" until you embrace a different mindset. Proverbs 5:1 says that a wise man will hear and increase learning. Be open to hear, receive, and embrace new ideas. These generally lead to an increase in skill, understanding, and wisdom—which usually translate into success!

The successful person of tomorrow is the one who is not afraid of change today.

The successful person of tomorrow is the one who is not afraid of change today. Begin challenging your mind to change and grow. Invest in yourself by enrolling in a class or listening to a daily podcast which can increase your efficiency. Learn something new, even if you're in the so-called "twilight" years of life. Embrace change. See yourself at a different level. Invest in yourself! You're worth it!

chapter 6

HOW TO WIN
AT WORK

*i*f you picked up this book expecting to see chapters entitled "How to Win the Lottery" or "Overnight Millions," then you might be a little disappointed to see an entire chapter dedicated to the subject of work. Contrary to some people's belief, "work" is not a foul four-letter word. In fact, it has everything to do with living the good life. To live this life to the fullest, you must understand how to not survive at a job, but rather how to win at work. It is a necessity.

And it is possible!

God has blessed each of us with the ability to work by giving us a heavenly endowment of unique gifts and talents. But somewhere along the way, the thought has been propagated that work is evil. One of the culprits in this misguided thinking stems from the constant barrage of television and social media ads. You know, the ones that seem to pop up every two minutes on your screen, buzzing with testimonials of people who have managed to amass enough money that they no longer are bothered with the hum-drum lifestyle which includes a j-o-b. They make it look so easy, sitting by the pool with a drink in their hand, surrounded by tanned beach bodies. Now, if you've purchased one of these "systems" but didn't experience million-dollar success, don't feel bad. Most folks who succumb to this temptation soon realize the ones getting rich are those selling the systems.

Media hounds aren't the only ones who have undermined the value of work—the super-spiritual have added to it, as well. These are the ones who argue, "If Eve hadn't blown it in the Garden, we would not have to toil and work like we do." Oh, really? It might do these folks some good to actually read the Bible. If they did, they would find that in the book of Genesis, someone was working long before Adam and Eve were ever alive on this planet.

His name is God.

How do you think God created this amazing planet? He worked. The Bible says that for six days, God created and on the seventh day, He rested (Genesis 2:2). But He didn't stop there. Not only did God institute the idea of work, but He also gave Adam a job tending the Garden right after forming him from the dust of the earth (Genesis 2:15). Have you ever noticed that the Lord gave Adam a job before giving him a wife? Before he could take care of someone, he had to take care of something. (That's for another book, entirely!)

Since work is God's idea and a huge component to success, let's examine some ways to not just survive at a job, but win at work.

WORK AND SUCCESS

From the beginning of time until now, success and work have always gone hand-in-hand. God was the pattern, and then He instructed us to follow suit by working six days and resting on the seventh (Exodus 20:9-10). The problem is, many Christians want to switch this equation and work one day while resting six. Then, they wonder why they never see increase or find favor. Not only that, these same people get mad at others who are rewarded for their hard work with blessings and increase. But those who are in pursuit of the good life recognize work for what God intended it to be: a channel of blessing.

Donald Kendall, the Co-founder of PepsiCo®, emphasized the proper alignment with work and success with his classic comment: "The only place where success comes before work is in the dictionary."[18]

The truth of this statement is timeless. If you want to succeed, you must first work—not just labor, but excel at what God has given you. Here are four powerful ingredients to help you connect God to your work.

1. Potential

The hidden treasures God has deposited into you—better known as your potential—must have a vehicle in which to flourish. It's called "work". When you work, your potential is released.

---

18 Greenwich Sentinel, "The Legend of PepsiCo Reflects on an Extraordinary Life," Greenwich Sentinel, 7 Septemember, 2015, https://www.greenwichsentinel.com/2015/09/07/donald-kendall-the-legend-of-pepsico-reflects-on-an-extraordinary-life/.

However, if you choose not to work, your God-given potential lays untapped and untouched. Always remember, God's original intent for what He has invested in you is to bring Him glory. Sure, you'll benefit when you exercise your potential; but ultimately, the reason for your talents and gifts is to "glorify your Father in heaven" (Matthew 5:16). Turn your potential into production.

2. Possibilities

Potential is what God has put in you. Possibilities—also known as opportunities—are what God has set before you. Just look at Adam, for example. God breathed life and potential into his nostrils and then placed the entire Garden under his command and authority.

Today, there is a garden of opportunity all around you. You merely need to find it. Even if you feel as though you're in a dead-end job, God may have placed you in that position to develop a specified trait and to build your character for a more significant opportunity yet to come. Maybe you're close to retirement and are looking to buy that RV and take off across the country. That's an awesome goal, as long as you keep looking for opportunities while cruising down the interstate! If you are well-able and well-minded, find something to do. It might be gardening, painting, writing a book, creating music, teaching children, or visiting the sick. There will always be an ample supply of opportunities available to those who are watching.

I once read about an African man who enrolled in elementary school at eighty-four years old. Up until then, he could never afford an education, but he seized his opportunity. He even cut off his slacks so he could wear shorts like the rest of the kids! It's never too late; if you are still breathing, God has opportunities and possibilities waiting for you.

3. Production. Work not only releases your potential, but it also activates your God-given energy and empowers you to produce. You're never going to exercise your dominion in the earth by sitting at home watching The View or scrolling through social media all day. Work is seeing a vision and applying your energies to bring it to pass.

God put you on this earth to produce, both naturally and spiritually. In the natural, diligence brings prosperity while laziness generates excuses. It takes work to transform dreams into reality. If your goal is to be wealthy, you must work in such a way to produce wealth.

Spiritually, work is the proof of faith. The Bible says that faith without any works is dead (James 2:26). If you say you have faith, then there must be the accompanying signs of deeds and work. Work is proof-positive of desire, and desires are fulfilled through the production of work.

Work not only releases your potential but it also activates your God-given energy and empowers you to produce.

4. Promise

Adam's unlimited potential and infinite possibilities to produce were all energized by another gift from God: His promise to multiply his efforts (Genesis 1:28). And His design has not changed. God's ultimate desire is that your time, energy, and talents be fruitful and multiply so as to satisfy you and bring Him all the glory.

You may be thinking, *What about the person who's lazy and doesn't use the abilities and talents God has given them?* Well, there's a promise for them, too.

> ". . . If anyone will not work, neither shall he eat."
> —2 Thessalonians 3:10

This scripture speaks of natural food and the broader need for fulfillment. It's true: A man who doesn't work is never fulfilled. On the other hand, the Bible says that when you till your land, you will have plenty of bread (Proverbs 28:19). When you put your hand to something, you are releasing God to bless it and bring the promise of fruitfulness and multiplication.

THE WINNING WAY

God never intended you to be poor; neither did He create you to be idle. Work is the key—winning at work is even better. Next are seven principles to help you enjoy the fruit of your labor and most importantly, please the Lord in your workplace. Apply these to your current situation and allow God to use your talents and gifts right where you are so He can bring you to where you're going.

Principle #1: Live and Work Like a Real Christian

Of all the seven principles, this is the most important because it should be every Christian's ultimate goal in life, not just in work. But for the sake of this chapter, we will concentrate on the work aspect.

If you think that Almighty God sent His only Son to this earth to be brutally murdered on a cross and then fight all the demons of hell so you can praise on Sunday and live like Satan Monday through Saturday, think again. The modern-day "Dr. Jekyll and Mr. Hyde" Christian will never enjoy real success. This is why working as a real Christian is not only vital to you but also to the message of the Kingdom to those with whom you share forty-plus hours a week.

To say you're a "Christian" means two things: 1) that you act like Christ, and 2) that you have an anointing on your life just as He did. Stop and ask yourself, "Do my co-workers see me as someone who works with godly integrity, character, commitment, and diligence? Am I productive with my time? Are my efforts producing fruit?" These are key elements to "acting like Christ" in the workplace.

Understand that as a child of God, you have an anointing on your life. Wherever God has assigned you—even in an adverse or hostile situation—He will anoint you. So, before you start complaining and looking for another job, start seeing God's hand right where you are. Believe you are anointed to function, operate, serve, and succeed right now in that position. Strive to fulfill your mission. Begin living and working as a real Christian and complete this mission given to you by the Lord.

Principle # 2: Accept Your Work as a Gift from God Rather than a Curse

"Back to the old grind." "Another day, another dollar." While these attitudes describe much of the workforce mentality, they never will contribute to your vocational success . . . but gratitude will. Seeing your work as a gift from God will change your attitude and productivity. Instead of cursing your job, begin thanking God every day for blessing you with it. Be thankful He has given you a productive way to spend your time, release your potential, and make some money!

Ninetieth Century English novelist and devout Christian, Charles Kingsley, penned these words:

> *Thank God every morning when you get up, that you have something to do that day which must be done, whether you like it or not. Being forced to work and forced to do your best will breed in you temperance and self-control, diligence and strength of will, cheerfulness and content, and a hundred virtues which the idle never know.*[19]

These words concur with Ecclesiastes 5:18-19:

> Here is what I have seen: It is good and fitting for one to eat and drink, and to enjoy the good of all his labor in which he toils under the sun all the days of his life which God gives him; for it is his heritage. As for every man to whom God has given riches and wealth, and given him power to eat of it, to receive his heritage and rejoice in his labor—this is the gift of God.

Your work is a gift from God. Rejoice in your labor. Receive your heritage. Be thankful and grateful for what God has given you. Have an attitude of gratitude, even when it pertains to your job. It will make all the difference in the world.

---

19 Charles Kingsley, Town and Country Sermons, "Work," Bible Hub, accessed September, 2023, https://biblehub.com/library/kingsley/town_and_country_sermons/sermon_xii_work.htm.

Principle #3: See God as Your True Employer

Now, before you phone into work one morning and say, "I will not be at work today. God gave me the day off," let me explain this section a bit further. Ephesians 6:5-8 (MSG) says this:

> Servants, respectfully obey your earthly masters but always with an eye to obeying the real master, Christ. Don't just do what you have to do to get by, but work heartily, as Christ's servants doing what God wants you to do. And work with a smile on your face, always keeping in mind that no matter who happens to be giving the orders, you're really serving God. Good work will get you good pay from the Master, regardless of whether you are slave or free.

Wherever God has assigned you— even in an adverse or hostile situation—He will anoint you.

These scriptures coincide with our first point—living and working as a real Christian. When you view God as your "boss", you will most likely be diligent about your work, whether your natural boss is around or not. Don't get caught in the trap of simply being an eye-pleaser. Work hard, even when no one is looking. If you have an office job, don't be on the phone with a friend until you hear your boss coming down the hall, and then act as though you were "busy" on your computer. If you have the privilege of working from home, work as though you were in the office surrounded by other employees. Even if your boss can't see you, or you are your own boss, remember that God is always watching.

These scriptures in the book of Colossians further accentuate this point:

> And whatever you do in word or deed, do all in the name of the Lord Jesus, giving thanks to God the Father through Him . . . Bondservants, obey in all things your masters according to the flesh, not with eyeservice, as men-pleasers, but in sincerity of heart, fearing God. And whatever you do, do it heartily, as to the Lord and not to men, knowing that from the Lord you will receive the reward of the inheritance; for you serve the Lord Christ. —Colossians 3:17, 22-24

The words "bondservant" and "master" can be translated as "employee" and "employer". In this light, the Bible again instructs employees to be faithful to their employers, never doing just enough to "get by", but instead to work hard from their heart as unto the Lord. When you recognize your true employer is God Almighty, then you will come into this powerful revelation: Even though your earthly employer may sign your check, he does not control your income.

If you will trust God and honor Him on your job, He will move on your behalf and honor you. And look at the promise at the end of the verses we just read: You will receive the reward of inheritance. I don't know about you, but for me, that's better than any paycheck, raise, or stock dividend. Payday isn't just on Fridays; it's eternal, as well.

Principle #4: Handle Your Business with the Right Attitude

This section could easily be entitled, "How to Freak Out Your Boss on Monday Morning!" I'm convinced if you apply these next steps, people will start scratching their heads and say, "Wow! What happened to you? I've never seen you like this since you came to work here." Call it what you may; either way, study and apply these three points on how to deal with your attitude and watch the reactions. Hey, you might even get that promotion you've been wanting.

> *Even though your earthly employer may sign your check, he does not control your income.*

Stop complaining. Do you know that when you complain, it's an insult to God? . . . considering He's your true employer! Many people work, but too few do so without complaining. I'm sure you've heard co-workers complain about being overworked, underpaid, overlooked, undertrained, taken advantage of, etc. We all have. But people who constantly complain very rarely see promotion, and thus never live a successful life.

The Bible says to "do all things without complaining or disputing" (Philippians 2:14). When you live a life free of whining and fault-finding, you become a breath of fresh air to everyone around you, and people see Jesus working through you.

Every difficulty is just an opportunity in disguise.

Do more than is expected of you. You can always spot those who live the mundane, day-to-day life. They're usually the ones with the "that's not my job," attitude when asked to do something outside their scope of responsibility. However, those who are pressing for the good life go the second mile . . . and maybe even the third, fourth, and fifth mile when needed.

If your boss asks you to compile a report, give him or her excellence beyond adequacy. Instead of handing in a few pieces of paper with an old coffee ring on the front, take some time to prepare a multi-page report in a color binder with the title on the front cover. Include some spreadsheets and maybe a PowerPoint™ presentation. Remember whose name you carry. Show your employer what it would be like to have Jesus working for them.

Work the environment. Contrary to what you might see on social media, there is no perfect place to work. Every job comes with its fair share of difficulties, mainly because other people work there. But instead of allowing your work environment to work you over, you can begin to work your environment and transform trouble into treasure.

Every difficulty is just an opportunity in disguise. Learn how to work with different personalities and situations. God will purposely put people in your life to complete His good work in you. Some will help you develop patience, while others sharpen your ability to love the unlovely. The important thing is to allow the Lord to use your environment to assist you in your spiritual and personal growth.

Walter Scott once said, "For success, attitude is equally as important as ability."[20] You can have talent running out of your ears, but without the right attitude, it will get you nowhere. Adjust your attitude to determine your altitude in life. Success and blessing are sure to follow.

Principle #5: Always Remember Your Mission

This might come as a surprise to you, so get ready. As Christians, we must continually remind ourselves that money is not our mission. Stay with me for a moment. We all understand the principle that "the laborer is worthy of his wages" (Luke 10:7), but as believers, money isn't our ultimate objective. The truth about money is: It will fund your mission, but money is not the mission. Wherever God has placed you is for a larger purpose than yourself. The Bible puts it this way:

> "You are the light of the world. A city that is set on a hill cannot be hidden. Nor do they light a lamp and put it under a basket, but on a lampstand, and it gives light to all who are in the house. Let your light so shine before men, that they may see your good works and glorify your Father in heaven."
> —Matthew 5:14-16

You are much more than an employee where you work—you are an ambassador for Christ. Ambassadors are highly-ranked

---

20 Walter Scott, "For success, attitude is equally as important as ability," BrainyQuote, 20 September, 2023, https://www.brainyquote.com/quotes/walter_scott_118620.

diplomats with full authority to speak for and represent their head of state in a foreign land. You, my friend, carry that responsibility for your "head of state"—Jesus—and characterize the Kingdom of God in your workplace. Do your best to represent the Lord daily in your words, actions, and deeds. Your mission is to exemplify the love of Christ, and people are watching.

Principle # 6: Be the Answer, Not the Problem

From budgets to buildings, personnel to public perception, and advertising to administration, every workplace has problems. It's part of being in business. But every problem has an answer. That's precisely why God placed you at your job—to be a resource of solutions. However, if you're always caught up in your environment, you may never see where you can provide assistance and answers. Many companies still exist and thrive today because Christians who work there have offered solutions that could have only come from the mind of God.

> *Money will fund your mission, but money is not the mission.*

While working in your designated position, always be mindful that God could use you to bring answers to issues that arise in different departments. Do you remember David in the Old Testament? After the Prophet Samuel anointed him, the Bible says the Spirit of God departed from King Saul, and he became distressed with an evil spirit (1 Samuel 16:14). Now, if you've been employed for any length of time, you know full well that when the boss isn't happy, nobody's happy. But David, a shepherd by trade, had the answer. Seeing that he was also an accomplished musician, David played his harp and the evil spirits vexing Saul left (1 Samuel 16:23).

When you are known as a "solver of problems", you become valuable not only to your employer but to yourself, as well. Always be looking for opportunities to help—even in unexpected places. Who knows, your data entry position right now might be your first step to Executive Assistant, then Vice President, then CEO. It worked for King David, and it can work for you.

Principle # 7: Stay Focused on the Future

If you're in a position right now that you don't like, don't give up. You're just passing through. This isn't the end goal for your life; it's just preparation for where God's taking you. Take the Apostle Paul's advice to forget what lies behind and reach forward to what lies ahead (Philippians 3:13).

Many times, these types of situations can be complicated and produce little motivation but let me encourage you that God is working His good pleasure in you (Philippians 2:13). Your eternal purpose and design are in His hands and where you are now is just a "checkpoint" for where you are going.

EVERYBODY WINS

Learning to win at work isn't just for your benefit, it can be a blessing for generations to come. Proverbs 13:22 says:

> "A good man leaves an inheritance to his children's children."

What an incredible promise—and responsibility. Plenty of people have heard or read this scripture and mentally agree with it, but it's not their reality. Friend, it takes much more than mental ascent and good intentions for this scripture to be fulfilled in your life. Many facets are required—one is learning how to win at work.

How can that happen? You can start by putting these principles to work:

» Work as a real Christian with a high emphasis on integrity and diligence.

» See your work as God's gift and treat it as such.

» Work as if God is your employer. He, in fact, really is.

» Stop complaining. Do more than what's expected of you.

» Work as an ambassador of the Kingdom of God.

» Offer solutions to problems.

» Don't be short-sighted. God has a plan, and you are just passing through to the next step.

Whether you're currently employed or are in the market for a job, these seven principles will transform your view regarding your work experience. Believe that God is directing your steps. Watch how God begins to move obstacles and promote you as you submit yourself to His job-training. Learn to walk in wisdom, redeem your time, and seize every opportunity for God's glory.

God is faithful to His promises, and He will reward your diligence with promotion. Trust Him to supernaturally direct your steps.

Wherever He leads, always know you can—and will—win at work!

chapter 7

THE TRUTH ABOUT MONEY

*i*f the title of this chapter made you uneasy, then you're exactly the one who needs to read it! If the enemy assaulted your mind with a negative thought missile, tempting you to skip to the next chapter, resist him—because chapter eight deals with money, too!

Throughout my life, money and sex have been two subjects considered extremely taboo to discuss in the Church. For hundreds of years, no minister dared to mention these two subjects from the pulpit, as they stood the risk of being shunned by their congregants. People in the pews often thought, *My money and my sex life are no one else's business!* Of course, maybe this explains why Christians have struggled in these areas for years.

It's time for a change.

Would you believe that Jesus talked more about money than heaven? It's true. The truth about money—specifically its significance, value, and purpose—is a subject God knows we all need to hear, live, and apply to our daily lives. The trouble has been the misrepresentation and misappropriation of these biblical truths. But just because someone has distorted or perverted the truth, does not make it any less authentic.

No matter what your mindset is about God and money, I believe these next few pages can revolutionize your thinking and allow you to live in a higher place in life. Look at it this way: If this subject is important to God (and it is!), then it should be significant to you, as well.

Let's dive into the truth about money.

TRUTH #1: GOD OWNS IT ALL

As obvious as this statement may be, it is and will forever be the truth. Everything belongs to God—the earth and everything in it, plus all of its wealth and resources. Consider these verses found in your Bible:

> "The silver is Mine, and the gold is Mine, says the Lord of hosts." —Haggai 2:8

> "For every beast of the forest is Mine, and the cattle on a thousand hills. I know all the birds of the mountains, and the wild beasts of the field are Mine." —Psalm 50:10-11

God is the very author of life and everything it beholds, but many people quickly forget this truth when they achieve some level of success. Every time someone says, "I built this multi-million-dollar organization," or "I make millions of dollars each year," what they really should be saying is, "God has helped me achieve this success." It's amazing how many who take the credit for their success were the same ones crying out to God for help during a time of bankruptcy or poverty!

God owns all the resources, but the Bible says that He is not stingy—that He gives you the power to create wealth (Deuteronomy 8:18). How does He empower you? Through your physical ability to work, your mental faculties which allow you to make sound decisions, and your innovations and creative abilities.

All of these come from God.

The author of it all isn't hoarding His creation or wealth upon Himself. Neither is He keeping it at arm's length from His children. It is available to you—right now!

TRUTH #2: MONEY IS A GIFT FROM GOD

Would you agree that having money is a good thing? Of course, it is. We need it to live our everyday lives, lay up an inheritance, and promote the gospel throughout the world. It's a good thing, and the Bible clearly states that every good thing in this life—including money—is a gift from God (James 1:17). The book of Ecclesiastes explains this in further detail:

> "As for every man to whom God has given riches and wealth, and given him the power to eat of it, to receive his heritage and rejoice in his labor—this is the gift of God." —Ecclesiastes 5:19

Did you see that? Riches and wealth are gifts from God! But God has never given anything to anyone without a defined purpose, intrinsic value, and eternal significance. This includes the gift of money. God's blessings of financial increase aren't just so you can buy another car, a bigger house, or have a nice vacation. There's nothing wrong with any of these, as long as you first understand God's specific purposes designated to your wealth.

The gift of money placed in your life is never just about you. Just like Abraham, you are blessed to be a blessing! (Genesis 12:2) This is one reason the favor of the Lord brings you to places where others can't go—even if they possess more skills and better criteria. Money is the original gift that keeps on giving!

> *The favor of the Lord brings you to places where others can't go—even if they possess more skills and better criteria.*

TRUTH #3: MONEY IS ESSENTIAL FOR LIFE

If you don't think money is a necessity for life, then do this simple exercise: Instead of getting dressed for work tomorrow morning, call your boss and say, "I'm not coming in today, tomorrow, or any other day! I quit. Take my cubicle and give it to someone else." Then, about a month later when you're knocking on people's doors asking for help to pay your electric bill, you'll see the importance of having money.

There's a scripture in the Bible concerning money that most Christians probably have never heard. Allow me to shed some light on it:

> "A feast is made for laughter, and wine makes merry; but money answers everything." —Ecclesiastes 10:19

I didn't make this up! It's in plain black and white: "Money answers everything." Notice the Bible doesn't say that money is the answer to all things; however, it is an essential fiber of our society, and survival without it would be extremely problematic, to say the least.

Have you ever noticed how the electric company likes to be paid for the power they provide to your house? How about the gas station or grocery store? Just try walking out of the store, not paying for your groceries, while saying, "Jesus paid it all!" You'll probably need money for bail soon!

Not only does God desire for you to pay your bills, but there's also the importance of saving and investing. The attitude of, "I just want enough to get by," isn't a mark of humility. What it really says is that you're selfish, stingy, and you don't value God's provisions for your life. Biblical economics will put you in a place where not only are your needs met, but you can be a financial blessing to others as well.

TRUTH #4: WEALTH IS MORE THAN MONEY

I've often heard it said that if you want to feel rich, start by counting the things you have that money can't buy. While the majority of society thinks wealth and money are synonymous, that is not always the case. Wealth encompasses far more than a healthy bank account, large retirement accounts, and profitable investments. Money alone can never ensure someone's inner peace, joy, mental health, emotional stability, salvation, righteousness, or the power of God working in their life. Those are some of the signs of true wealth.

In Acts 3:6, two of Jesus' disciples, Peter and John, were on their way to church. At the Gate called Beautiful, they encountered a crippled beggar who was asking for a handout. Peter's response proved that wealth was more than money, as he said, "Silver and gold I do not have, but what I do have I give you: In the name of Jesus Christ of Nazareth, rise up and walk." This beggar asked for money, but instead received healing—a wealth that changed his destiny forever!

> *Wealth encompasses far more than a healthy bank account, large retirement accounts, and profitable investments.*

TRUTH #5: MONEY IS A MEASURE

By definition, the word "money" simply means "something generally accepted as a medium of exchange, a measure of value, or a means of payment."[21] If you ever travel overseas, you'll find an amazing fact: You need money in every country for survival.

---

21 Merriam-Webster Dictionary, s.v. "money," accessed September, 2023, https://www.merriam-webster.com/dictionary/money.

Whether it is an American dollar, a British pound, a Mexican peso, a Japanese yen, or a Russian ruble—money is a means of payment.

What makes money valuable isn't the amount you have in your wallet or bank account, but the value it represents. For example, a million US dollars can go much further than a million pesos or rupees. In that light, obtaining a millionaire status is all relevant to the currency in which it is based. Altogether, money in and of itself is simply the measure of what you pay, not the measure of your personal financial status.

TRUTH #6: MONEY IS A TOOL

We live in a day when the Kingdom of God is expanding at a record pace. Daily, people are turning their hearts to Jesus and accepting His grace and forgiveness into their lives. One reason for this evangelical explosion is the fact that people are hearing the gospel now more than ever through television, the Internet, streaming video, conference calls, mass evangelistic crusades, etc. One thing all of these have in common: They cost money to be effective!

Television time is not free, neither are plane tickets nor living expenses for missionaries in foreign lands. I don't know any Consulate from another country that has greeted gospel missionaries with free housing, food, and a supply of money to live.

Where does this money come from?

From people like you and I who see money as a tool.

Here's the caveat: If you're broke and are living on "Barely-Get-By Street," you have no money to give towards missionary works around the world! The commandment given to the Church is to preach the gospel of the Kingdom to every nation, tribe, tongue, and person on this earth—and it takes money to do so.

Not only is money a necessity in spreading the Gospel around the world, but it's also a tool in which to make wealth. The adage, "It takes money to make money" is entirely true. Living from paycheck to paycheck is a challenging task, but this kind of life is more of an improper mindset than a money issue. I know people who make crazy amounts of money and still live week-to-week. They have no fiscal discipline and are consumers—buying everything they can even if they don't need it or can't afford it.

> *Money isn't something you only spend; it's a tool you can use.*

On the other hand, I've known people who make much less income yet retire with hundreds of thousands of dollars in the bank. They accomplished this by being disciplined to consistently deposit money into savings or retirement accounts over several years. In the end, their money worked for them instead of them working for their money.

In Deuteronomy 8:13, God told the children of Israel that all they had—gold, silver, herds, flocks—would multiply. Today, we call this the law of compound interest, and it's one of the most remarkable tools for acquiring wealth over a period of time. Money isn't something you only spend; it's a tool you can use. Put it to work and watch God bless your efforts.

TRUTH #7: MONEY HAS A VOICE

I once heard an elderly man say, "It's true, money talks. I had a dollar bill once, and it said 'Goodbye!'" Even though this was a funny spin, the truth remains—money does talk. If you don't believe it, then walk to the maître d' at a restaurant and start flipping out some $100 bills! It won't be long before, "I'm so sorry, sir, there is no seating available," changes to, "I see where there's one table opening up. Right this way."

Money has always carried influence. It always will. For the most part, people typically will not listen to someone who is poor. Even if a poor person has good advice, it usually doesn't carry much clout or influence. Ecclesiastes 9:13-16 tells a story where a poor man, by using his wisdom, actually saved a city from a king who sieged it. Sadly, the Scriptures also say, "No one remembered that same poor man." It's still true: People will listen to someone who's rich over the counsel of the poor—even if the rich give wrong advice!

The voice of money is both good and bad. There's a little word called "debt" that she screams, usually through the avenue called credit cards. Have you ever heard that voice coming out of your wallet or purse—usually at the time when you really want something but know you can't afford it? The credit card says, "Hey, go ahead. Get it. Charge it. You deserve it. You know you can pay it off at the end of the month. That's what I'm here for—to help you through these tough times." Before long, that card is maxed out and you're applying for another one to pay it off. Stop the madness! If you've found yourself in bondage to these "wonderful little blessings," it may be time to take out the scissors and do some "plastic surgery"—and the sooner, the better.

Money speaks. In the hands of the unrighteous, it can speak greed, poverty, and debt; but in the hands of the righteous, money can speak of blessing and increase.

ANOTHER TRUTH

While we're discovering the truth about money, let's go ahead and unveil another controversial subject in the body of Christ: prosperity. Over the last thirty years, there has been much teaching concerning Biblical prosperity, to the point that it feels like thirty-one flavors at a Baskin Robbins® store! At the risk of being "flavor number thirty-two," allow me to share what I believe the definition of true biblical prosperity is: having enough of God's supply to complete His assignment for your life.

True prosperity is having enough of God's supply to complete His assignment for your life.

Did you notice a word missing in this definition? Money! That's because true prosperity is more about your assignment and purpose than your money. Don't get me wrong; you'll need an ample supply of resources to complete God's assignment for your life, but your life-long dream and vision from God are far more valuable than money can ever buy. The Bible says that without a vision, people dry up and die (Proverbs 29:18 author paraphrase). You can have all the money in the world, but without a God-breathed vision and purpose to attach it to, you are not prospering.

Which brings me to another subject: poverty.

Poverty is not necessarily being broke, but rather not having enough to complete your God-given mission on this earth. When God tells you to do something, He will never withhold the resources to bring it to pass. The problem isn't with God; it's with Christians learning how to tap into God's divine flow. I can firmly assure you that God's not going to wave a magic wand over your head that automatically produces the winning Powerball lottery numbers! He's given you something much better: gifts, talents, and abilities to create the wealth you need to complete your assignment.

Godly prosperity not only brings you joy, but it makes the Lord rejoice as you magnify Him in your prosperity. Psalm 35:27 says:

> "Let them shout for joy and be glad, who favor my righteous cause; and let them say continually, 'Let the Lord be magnified, who takes pleasure in the prosperity of His servant.'"

What child of God wouldn't want his Heavenly Father to take pleasure in their life? One way to accomplish this is by living a life of prosperity—a life enriched with peace and abundance. Over the years, I've had people ask me, "Pastor, can someone poor bring glory to God?" The answer is, "Yes." Christians have been doing that for years. But there's a better way! The psalmist David described it this way:

> "Praise the Lord! Blessed is the man who fears the Lord, who delights greatly in His commandments. His descendants will be mighty on earth; the generation of the upright will be blessed. Wealth and riches will be in his house, and his righteousness endures forever." —Psalms 112:1-3

What is supposed to be in your house? Wealth and riches, not ants and roaches! (If you have ants and roaches, remember "money answers everything," and it will pay for an exterminator!)

The life of prosperity is not an overnight, one-time thing. It's a lifelong journey. Start where you are, right now. If you're not enjoying this kind of life, don't fall into the mindset that this is your "lot in life." That's a lie of the devil. On the other hand, maybe you've experienced a life of prosperity, but bad decisions or a lack of good judgment have caused you to fail. Admit your mistakes, ask God for forgiveness, and don't stay there! Get up, dust yourself off, and get back on track.

Deuteronomy 8:7 says that God is bringing you into a good land, a land without scarcity or lack so to bring glory to His name. Prosperity awaits you. God has given you the power, ability, and authority to gain wealth. Now, you can run your race to the fullest . . .

. . . with money in your bank account!

chapter 8

MONEY MYTHS

*t*hey've been around since the second century B.C. and have turned fictional characters like Hercules and Zeus into gods and heroes. They have kept children wondering things like, "If I swallow gum, will it stay in my stomach for seven years?" Their cast of characters includes Paul Bunyan, Jack and the Beanstalk, Bigfoot, and the Loch Ness monster. What are they? Myths!

The American Heritage Dictionary describes myths as, "A fiction or half-truth, especially one that forms part of an ideology."[22] Everyone knows what a half-truth is, right? A whole lie! Myths are mostly far-fetched from reality, but on occasion, they can be laden with some truth—which makes them even more dangerous.

Myths are not only connected to fairy tales and larger-than-life legends, but they also exist in the real world. One of their most

---

22 American Heritage Dictionary, s.v. "myth," September, 2023, https://www.ahdictionary.com/word/search.html?q=myths&submit.x=0&submit.y=0.

dominant areas of influence is in the subject of money—particularly with Christians. Too many people have taken bits and pieces of scripture and manufactured their own versions of what the Bible says about money. No wonder the Bible very explicitly states that God's people die—not only physically, but spiritually, emotionally, and financially—because they lack knowledge and understanding (Hosea 4:6).

That's about to change.

Before there's a change in your checking account, there must be a change in between your temples. It's time to invalidate the religious theories and traditions about money and come to a better understanding of what the Bible truly says. Let's expose these myths, starting with the one most commonly believed.

> *Before there's a change in your checking account, there must be a change in between your temples.*

MYTH #1: MONEY IS EVIL

If there has ever been a belief concerning money which is a half-truth, it's this one. People have been saying this for centuries, but it's simply not true. Why don't we take a look at what the Bible really says:

> "For the love of money is a root of all kinds of evil . . ."
> —1 Timothy 6:10

As previously stated, money in and of itself is not evil. Though it is not inherently righteous or evil, money will always take on the characteristics—or spirit—of the one handling it. The money used to send missionaries to foreign lands could also be the same money used to fund a drug addiction in someone else's control. Same money, different conduit, different results.

> *. . . Money will always take on the characteristics—of spirit— of the one handling it.*

Have you ever noticed that godliness is not a requirement to have money? The Bible clearly states that sinners have wealth (Proverbs 13:22b)—sometimes, a lot of it. I can't count the number of times I've seen someone who was a sinner and "loaded" get saved and then go broke. Somewhere down the road, they succumbed to the thought that having money was wrong. I've always wanted to ask them, "Why not turn those resources (which usually have been used on unrighteous living) into a force for the gospel? God is the One who gave it to you, so use it for His glory and honor."

Money is like electricity in that the same power that warms your house can also burn your home to the ground. The difference is in how it's handled.

MYTH #2: MONEY IS UNSPIRITUAL

Whenever someone comes to me and says, "Pastor, how dare you talk about my money in church," it's a sure sign that money—not God—controls their life. These people believe that money is not a spiritual matter; thus, it should not be addressed within the confines of the church. Well, if this is true, then why is it directly mentioned more than 800 times in the Bible? Not to mention the more than 2,000 references to finances in general! I think it's clear: Money is indeed very spiritual, and it needs to be dealt with as such.

One of the ways money is spiritual is the fact that it represents you—a spirit being. Jesus said that your money is a direct reflection of your heart (Matthew 6:21). If you want to see your priorities in life, just look at where you spend your money. Judas, the disciple who betrayed Jesus, is a perfect example. Money—not political prestige, social fame, or a governmental seat—exposed his heart. Judas followed the money . . . all the way to his suicidal death.

Money is also spiritual because it's one of your truest acts of worship. Mark 12:43 tells of an incident where Jesus Himself stood outside the treasury, taking note of everyone who gave and their amount. The widow who gave two little coins out of her poverty was the only one who caught His attention that day. Jesus commended her for her incredible sacrifice by telling His disciples that she had put in more than anyone else who gave that day.

Malachi 3:10 gives another example of money's link to spirituality. The Bible says:

> "'Bring all the tithes into the storehouse, that there may be food in My house, and try Me now in this,' says the LORD of hosts, 'If I will not open for you the windows of heaven and pour out for you such blessing that there will not be room enough to receive it.'"

According to this scripture, money—or more specifically, the giving of money—is one way to unlock spiritual blessings.

There are many other ways money is connected to your spiritual life. It can create relationships that can be helpful or detrimental to your spiritual life. Money, like your spiritual life, can expand and grow. Hopefully, you pray (a spiritual act) often for God's blessings—including money—on your life and the ones you love. Here again, the two are connected.

There is no doubt that money is scriptural. The quicker you accept that fact, the better you will see how the connection can be a blessing, not a curse, in your life.

MYTH #3: MONEY GUARANTEES HAPPINESS

Jesus called this myth the "deceitfulness of riches" (Matthew 13:22). If money could really buy happiness, then every rich person on the planet would never have a day of anxiety or worry. The sad truth is that our news feeds are filled several times a year with reports of yet another rich and famous person who tragically took their own life. It brings Jesus' words to light, "For what will it profit a man if he gains the whole world, and loses his soul?" (Mark 8:36)

Money can never guarantee happiness because money is fleeting. There's a reason why the phrase "Money comes, and money goes," has been passed down for generations. Because it's true. Proverbs 23:5 says that money flies away like an eagle toward heaven. You can almost hear people chasing it down screaming, "Come back! Come back! Money, please come back!"

True happiness in this life only comes through one thing: a personal relationship with Jesus Christ. If you're a Christian, then here's the good news: You can have a lot of money and be happy at the same time. God never says that you must choose one or the other. If you love the Lord your God with all your heart, soul, mind, and strength, God will bless you with eternal happiness and money to boot.

MYTH #4: MONEY COMES TO SOME AND AVOIDS OTHERS

When you consider that roughly 48 percent of today's billionaires inherited at least a portion of their wealth, it can give this myth some legitimacy—that there are those who are born with a silver spoon in their mouths. But let's go back further than someone's wealthy father or grandfather . . . all the way back to the One who created everything.

The Bible clearly states that God is not a respecter of persons (James 2:1; Acts 10:34). What this means is that what He has for one, He has for all. God's not in the business of making some people live in poverty while others enjoy prosperity. Yet, people believe things like, "It's just my lot in life to be poor." This is, once again, a lie from the enemy to entrap people from living in the abundance God intended.

The truth is that everybody started with nothing; the difference is that some people learned how to prosper, even passing their fortunes on to future generations, and some didn't.

The world is full of "rags to riches" stories. Take movie mega-star Jim Carrey as an example. Born in Ontario, Canada, Carrey's parents worked janitorial and security night jobs to make ends meet. Eventually, his family was forced out of their home and had to live in their camper van. This didn't stop the aspiring actor from pursuing his dreams. Today, Jim Carrey is one of the highest-paid comedians and actors in Hollywood.

Business mogul Wayne Huizenga used his childhood abuse from his father to motivate him towards a better life. After attending college for a short stint, Huizenga enlisted in the Army reserves where he trained for about a year. After his army training, Wayne moved to Florida where he purchased one garbage truck and began collecting trash in a growing community. In less than ten years, that one garbage truck grew into the largest waste management company in the United States, Waste Management, Inc.®. But he wasn't done there.

This Irish-born immigrant also founded Blockbuster Video®, Auto Nation®, and was the owner of three professional sports teams before his death in 2018. Huizenga was the recipient of the "2005 World Entrepreneur of the Year" award.

Born to unwed, teenage parents in Mississippi, this young lady was raised by her grandmother until the age of six. Being poor and not able to provide much, her grandmother did offer this child one great asset—the ability to read before the age of three. This skill catapulted her to excel in school, eventually earning her a scholarship to attend a private high school.

As she grew older, this teenage girl ran away from home and moved to live with her father in Tennessee. There, she took her first media job as a part-time news reporter at a local, African

American radio station. Sensing this was her passion in life, this up-and-coming star worked as the youngest news anchor in the history of WLAC-TV in Nashville, Tennessee, and then moved to Baltimore, Maryland where she anchored the six o'clock news and co-hosted a local talk show called *People Are Talking*[23].

It wasn't long before this up-and-comer became one of the top attractions for national television producers, which moved her to Chicago to host AM Chicago. Within a few months, Oprah Winfrey turned the very low-rated morning show into the highest-ranked talk show in all of Chicago. The show was renamed The Oprah Winfrey Show and enjoyed top-tier rankings for many years. Today, Ms. Winfrey is consistently listed as one of the wealthiest women in the world, owning many successful organizations including her production company, magazine, and cable network.

If you have fallen into the trap and believe the lie that money is avoiding you, it's time to change your thinking. God's plan for prosperity and wealth is for you, today. Change your, "Woe is me," thinking to, "I'm a child of the Most High God, and all my Father has for me is mine!"

Money is not avoiding you. In fact, if you take God at His Word and activate the proper principles, it will be running towards you.

You can have a lot of money and be happy at the same time.

---

23 Winfrey, Oprah, host. *People Are Talking*, Aired 1978, WJZ TV.

THREE KEYS

Myths about money are numerous, but there are also some common thoughts that are true. One that comes to mind is: Money doesn't grow on trees. In most cases, this sentiment is used by a weary father explaining to his children the difficulties of having enough resources to live. But the truth of this statement reaches much farther.

Waiting for money to magically bud out of a backyard tree makes about as much sense as playing the lottery. Wealth isn't the "luck of the draw". It comes by gaining a revelation, developing a plan, and putting that plan into practice. If you're serious about living the good life, then examine how these three keys can help get you there.

1. Decisions

Newsflash: Everything in life starts with a choice. You didn't wake up one day and, BAM, you were married! No, it began with a decision. In the same fashion, people who are wealthy decided to pursue wealth—and then put their hand to the plow and worked.

Let me give you an example of the power one decision holds. So many people have been renters their entire adult life. Several factors could influence this decision: fear of commitment, their parents never owned a home, fear that they can't qualify, etc. I've actually heard some people spiritualize their decision to rent by saying something like, "Well, I need to be mobile and ready to move anytime God says move." Twenty-five years later, God still hasn't moved them, and in the meantime, they made their landlord very wealthy. Just think how that same family could have benefited from purchasing a home instead of renting for all those years.

On the other hand, I know one particular woman who decided to purchase a home back in the sixties for $25,000 (That was a lot of money back then.) Some years later, due to her age and some health issues, she had to sell it . . . for $695,000! What a blessing. But it all started with a single choice many years ago.

If the fear of losing money or an inferiority complex due to your lack of education has paralyzed your financial life, it's time to make a decision to change. God is committed to your success. Start where you are. Begin making sound financial decisions, today, and watch God prosper your efforts.

2. Diligence

Spiritual laws—the law of faith, the law of sowing and reaping, the law of sin and death, etc.—never change. Here's one you might not know exists: the law of poverty. That's right. It's found in Proverbs 6:10-11:

> "A little sleep, a little slumber, a little folding of the hands to sleep—so shall your poverty come on you like a prowler, and your need like an armed man."

The law is simple: No matter how many right decisions you make, if you're lazy, poverty will show up on your doorstep. Laziness is not regulated to sitting on the couch watching Netflix all day; it also deals with work habits. Those who come in late, never do anything outside their job description, and never stay one minute past quitting time (even if there's work to be done) are "folding their hands." The law doesn't vacillate. Poverty is coming to their house.

But what about those who show up early and are very diligent about their work? These are the ones who position themselves for blessing and increase. The Bible says to consider the ant (Proverbs 6:6). Here's a creature that doesn't require any supervision or a time clock yet works meticulously to prepare for the future. That's diligence, and that leads to blessings.

3. Discipline

Ah, the word no one likes to hear. The word that gets you up an extra hour early in the mornings to have quiet time with the Lord or go to the gym. The word that keeps you in school to finish your degree while others drop out. It's the word that makes you cook at home and not spend your child's college education fund on fast-food restaurants. In the financial world, this word truly does separate the men from the boys, the "has" from the "has nots", the winners from the losers.

One of the easiest ways to exercise discipline in the area of finances is to start a savings account. This is nothing that hasn't been said numerous times, but still millions of families across the United States have very little, if any savings at all. It takes discipline to make it happen.

Start where you are. If you're broke, then $500 is quite a bit of money to have in savings. Most financial advisors (of which I am not one) will tell you to set a goal of saving six months of your salary in a separate account. That's right, six months—not six days or weeks! Deuteronomy 28 refers to it as your "storehouse." This is not the normal bills you pay, but a store where you can save.

None of these principles come easy, but to accomplish any goal, you must first start. Psalm 66:12 says that there is a wealthy place reserved just for you. Start now seeing yourself in that place. Begin to speak wealth and riches into your house, family, business, and future. Welcome them as a friend and companion on your life's journey.

If you're in a place where lack has controlled your life, stop right here and pray this prayer:

> *"Father God, I thank You for providing everything I need in this life. I desire to walk in the realm of financial freedom that You have ordained for me to enjoy. Lord, help me to change my mind so that I can be free to serve You in my fullest capacity. Thank You for blessing me so I can live without limitation, without restriction, and be able to participate in every good work for Your glory and Your honor. I believe I receive this now, in Jesus' name."*

Start seeing yourself as God sees you. Believe what the Bible says about you. Stop believing the myths that Satan and the religious-minded have tried to put on God's people for years. Just like Hercules and the Loch Ness Monster—they are a fantasy in someone's mind. God's Word, on the other hand, is real, true, and is setting you free to live the life He has planned for you.

It's called the good life.

chapter 9

TRUE RICHES

With an estimated net worth of close to $80 billion, Warren Buffett ranks as Forbes' 2023 fifth richest people in the world. While he clearly knows a thing or two about making money, perhaps his most important discovery is that money is not the most valuable asset one can own. Take a look at Buffet's philosophy as expressed in a memoir written by Alice Schroedertold:

> *Basically, when you get to my age, you'll really measure your success in life by how many of the people you want to have love you actually do love you.*
>
> *I know people who have a lot of money, and they get testimonial dinners, and they get hospital wings named after them. But the truth is that nobody in the world loves them. If you get to my age in life and nobody thinks well of you, I don't care how big your bank account is, your life is a disaster.*

That's the ultimate test of how you have lived your life. The trouble with love is that you can't buy it. You can buy sex. You can buy testimonial dinners. You can buy pamphlets that say how wonderful you are. But the only way to get love is to be lovable. It's very irritating if you have a lot of money. You'd like to think you could write a check: "I'll buy a million dollars' worth of love." But it doesn't work that way. The more you give love away, the more you get.[24]

Obviously, the 1964 Beatles' smash hit was right: "You Can't Buy Me Love." And there's a long list of other things money can never buy, as well. Why is this? Because there are things in this life far more valuable than money.

KNOW THE DIFFERENCE

We have already seen where Psalm 112:3 promises those who honor God "wealth and riches." These two words, even though often clumped into the same basket, have vastly different meanings.

» Wealth relates to multiple, sustainable possessions.
» Riches typically refer to money, equivalent means of exchange, or barter; and also consist of things far more valuable than money.

The Bible records an incident where Jesus addressed these two, in a story referred to as "The Rich Young Ruler." This young man's question to Jesus was simple: "What shall I do that I may inherit eternal life?" (Mark 10:17) Jesus first tells him that he should keep the commandments, which the young man confirms that he has. That was step one. However, Jesus' next requirement presented a much more difficult challenge:

24 Alice Schroeder, The Snowball: Warren Buffet and the Business of Life (New York: Bantam Books, 2008).

> "Then Jesus, looking at him, loved him, and said to him, 'One
> thing you lack: Go your way, sell whatever you have and give
> to the poor, and you will have treasure in heaven; and come,
> take up the cross, and follow Me.'" —Mark 10:21

Notice the Bible says that Jesus loved this young man—and
he had money. The same is true today. Jesus still loves all people
unconditionally and equally. But in this incident, it was Jesus'
love that allowed Him to look into a young man's soul and see
an incomplete person. What did Jesus see? The truth that all the
money in the world can never fill the void in someone's heart.

That truth remains today.

Even though Jesus addressed this young man's wealth, money was
never the root issue. His obedience, not his possessions, was being
tested. This heart check confirmed the young man's frail condition:

> "But he was sad at this word, and went away sorrowful, for he
> had great possessions." —Mark 10:22

Did this young man have money? Undoubtedly. Was he rich?
Apparently not. But it doesn't have to be this way. You can have both!
Having a knowledge of the Word and obedience to it are the keys.

THE KEY WORD

After this young man walked away, Jesus turned to His disciples and spoke what I believe to be one of the most grossly mis-
interpreted Scriptures found in the New Testament. The Lord
explained the situation by saying:

> "How hard it is for those who have riches to enter the kingdom
> of God!" —Mark 10:23

For years, the Church at large has used this Scripture to validate a doctrine of poverty that says, "If you're rich, you can't make it into heaven." Sad to say, many Christians—not knowing the truth of God's plan for abundance and blessing—have bought into this erroneous teaching and therefore lived far beneath God's best.

It's time to change.

Follow me here. If money were a hindrance to going to heaven, then Abraham would not be there. Neither would David, Solomon, Moses, or the disciples. Why? Because they all had money. Actually, after hearing these words of Jesus, the disciples were completely taken aback and confused. Maybe they began asking themselves, "I wonder if we're going to have to sell everything we own, too!" But Jesus quickly clarified the criteria by saying:

> "Children, how hard it is for those who trust in riches to enter
> the kingdom of God!" —Mark 10:24

Notice the difference: trust. Friend, the issue isn't that you have money; the issue is, do you trust in your wealth or do you trust in your God? The Apostle Paul warned his young pastor protégé, Timothy, to command those who are rich to not trust in uncertain riches, but in the living God. The question now is, "Is your strength found in the Lord your God or your 401k and stock portfolio?" Wealth and riches are yours for the taking, as long as you remember to "trust in the Lord with your heart" (Proverbs 3:5-6).

THE REAL THING

It's been well established throughout this book that money alone does not equal happiness or true wealth. Those only come from a life that is surrendered to Jesus and full of His forgiveness, grace, peace, and joy. Jesus made this clear, as well, in a very interesting statement found in Luke 16:11:

> "Therefore if you have not been faithful in the unrighteous mammon, who will commit to your trust the true riches?"

Notice the last two words, "true riches." It's clear that Jesus does not categorize money (unrighteous mammon) with what really counts in life—and you shouldn't either. Look at how this verse reads in the CJB:

"So if you haven't been trustworthy in handling worldly wealth, who is going to trust you with the real thing?"

. . . The issue is, do you trust in your wealth or do you trust in your God?

I don't know about you, but having only worldly wealth isn't enough for me. As someone once said, "The real measure of your wealth is how much you'd be worth if you lost all your money." True success can only be obtained with true riches—real treasures that reach beyond bank accounts and investment strategies (even though those are good, too). So, let's take a few minutes and examine some things that fall into Jesus' definition of "true riches."

#1: Knowing the Living God

We used to sing a song back in the day that said, "You can have this whole world but give me Jesus."[25] It's interesting to see how Christians with very little material possessions can sing this song with much more conviction than those believers with money in the bank! I'm not being mean or judgmental; it's just the truth.

To know God through a relationship with His Son, Jesus Christ is the highest asset you could ever obtain. No amount of money in the world can match the benefits that come from knowing God . . . and Him knowing you. Money will come and go. Life is a journey of seasons of plenty and times of scarcity. But through it all, when you have Jesus, you always have more than enough.

After pastoring for thirty-three years, you can only imagine how many times I've heard someone say, "All this church is after is my money!" I usually smile and say, "God doesn't want your money, He wants you—all of you. And when He has all of you, He already has your money!"

A real, flourishing, loving relationship with your Creator—the One who created you to enjoy all the benefits of life—is far more valuable than any amount of money. He is your source, your sustenance of life, your inheritance, and your portion of peace, favor, health, strength, and divine protection. It's easy to see why David encourages us to "taste and see that the Lord is good" (Psalm 34:8).

Because He is.

25 Selah (featuring Jack and Molly Smith), "I Have Decided to Follow Jesus" by Simon Kara Marak, track #10 on *You Deliver Me*, Curb Records. Inc.

#2: Having a Good Name

Some names in this world need no defining. Names like Gates, Hilton, Bezos, Zuckerberg, and Buffet are synonymous with great wealth. Washington, Lincoln, Roosevelt, Kennedy, Bush, and Obama are well-known presidents. Everyone knows these names, but are they "good names"? What about Hitler, Stalin, Manson, Madoff, and Dahmer? Again, all recognizable, but are they "good"?

What makes a good name?

It comes down to two issues: character and integrity. People like Billy Graham, Mother Teresa, Nelson Mandela, and Oral Roberts all have earned positive reputations through a lifetime of pursuing integrity and character. Never mistake your persona—how people perceive you in public by your character—the person you are when no one's around. The latter is what will set you apart as one with a stellar reputation.

How valuable are these "true riches"? King Solomon said it this way:

> "A good name is to be chosen rather than great riches, loving favor rather than silver and gold." —Proverbs 22:1

A good name is priceless mainly due to one reason: Opportunities opened by your talent can only be sustained by your integrity. It's true; your reputation does proceed you. Good or bad, it speaks volumes. With this said, a good name can grant you access to places that money could never afford.

Guarding and protecting your good name is priceless because once it's lost, it's practically irretrievable. In William Shakespeare's play Othello, even the foul villain Iago understood the significance of a good name:

> *"Good name in man and woman, dear my lord, is the immediate jewel of their souls. Who steals my purse steals trash . . . But he that filches from me my good name robs me of that which not enriches him and makes me poor indeed."*[26]

Your name may never be synonymous with power, fame, or money. That's okay. These have never been—and never will be—qualifications for a good reputation. The good news is this: You can have both a good name and money. In fact, they both can work together to set you in a place of prosperity and increase.

#3: Wisdom

It has been said that a fool and his money will soon depart. Thus, the value of godly wisdom. The wisest man to ever live penned it like this:

> "Wisdom is the principal thing; therefore get wisdom. And in all your getting, get understanding." —Proverbs 4:7

Stating this scripture in today's vernacular might sound like this: "In all of your effort to obtain money, wealth, connections, and contracts, don't forget to obtain the wisdom on what to do with them once you have them."

Can you imagine what some people would do if Almighty God Himself personally told them: "Ask me for anything you want, and I will give it to you."? Their minds would be racing! Money, riches,

---

26 Shakespeare, *Othello*, lines 155-161, Act 3, Scene 3.

fame, possessions, inheritance, etc. would roll through their thoughts like a slot machine. What you may not realize is, God did give King Solomon this opportunity, and look what he chose:

> "Now give me wisdom and knowledge, that I may go out and come in before this people . . ." —2 Chronicles 1:10a

Wait a minute. No riches? No fame? No great kingdom? No victory in battles? Only wisdom and knowledge? What was Solomon thinking? Did this great man just squander the greatest opportunity of his life? Not hardly. God granted his request . . . and a whole lot more:

> ". . . wisdom and knowledge are granted to you; and I will give you riches and wealth and honor, such as none of the kings have had who were before you, nor shall any after you have the like." —2 Chronicles 1:12

Talk about hitting the jackpot! Solomon got it all—supernatural wisdom and knowledge plus more wealth than any other person on earth.

Godly wisdom did not stop with Solomon. The same understanding that led Solomon into great victories and established him as the most predominate king of all time is available for you, today.

Walking in the wisdom of God enables you to see things no one else sees and know things no one else knows. Stock markets and money accounts will come and go, but godly wisdom will never diminish in value. Money flourishes when it follows wisdom.

Don't seek money; go beyond and pursue the "true riches" of wisdom. Your life will be eternally changed.

#4: A Good Spouse

I know some might disagree with this point, using the "You don't know what this man/woman has put me through," as ammunition. But look what the Bible says about the matter:

> "He who finds a wife finds a good thing, and obtains favor from the LORD." —Proverbs 18:22

Notice that the Bible says "good", not a "perfect" spouse. Why? Because one does not exist! So, what is a "good spouse"? Well, in my years of experience, I've never seen a mail-order bride, club hook-up, or sugar daddy qualify as "good". I'm not saying that they're not out there, but if you're single and fishing, be sure to drop your line in the right pond.

There are many reasons why a good spouse is more valuable than money. Let's look at just a few.

They enrich your life with incalculable blessings. No one can ever put a price tag on peace. And of all the peace found in this world, nothing is quite as soothing as a peaceful home. The peace and confidence knowing your home is in order brings heightened energy, time, and the ability to focus on other things—like making money.

How much is it worth for a man to be married to a woman in whom he completely trusts her judgment, counsel, love, and fidelity? It's priceless. In the same manner, the woman who knows her husband loves her unconditionally—giving his very life for her if need be—is empowered to be the woman God has called her to be. These assets added to one's life carry intrinsic value far beyond any amount of money.

The two become one. The Bible describes a married couple as being "one flesh." This doesn't mean that one completely loses their identity and becomes overtaken by the other. Rather, both parties, united with their individual creativity, passion, and love, form one union thus doubling the effectiveness of each individual. Deuteronomy 32:30 says that while one can put a thousand to flight, two will be able to put ten thousand to flight. That's the power of the union of two spirits.

A marriage that is flowing together, much like two streams that flow into one river, is a force more valuable than riches. When you and your spouse are walking together in agreement and harmony of purpose, the Bible says that your prayers will not be hindered (1 Peter 3:7). That, my friend, is a quality and assurance of life no money could ever buy.

#5: God's Word

Living the good life is not possible without the Word of God. The Psalmist David knew the value of God's Word:

> "The law of Your mouth is better to me than thousands of coins of gold and silver." —Psalm 119:72

Before you ever earned your degrees, charted your career path, accepted that big promotion, patented your invention, wrote your best-seller, planned your retirement, or made your millions, God's Word was already in existence. The Bible says: "In the beginning was the Word" (John1:1-3). The Word of God is the sustenance of life and the foundation of your success. Jesus understood this principle very clearly as He rebutted His tempter: "... 'Man shall not live by bread alone, but by every word that proceeds from the mouth of God'" (Matthew 4:4). These words still ring true today. The abundant life God has provided for you originated in a spiritual dimension and can never be solely obtained by the power of your flesh.

The power of the Word trumps the power of money every single time. If you're sick, money can buy you medicine, but the Word can heal your body. Money can retain the services of a good attorney, but the Word is your ultimate defense and advocate. Your money can put you into a position of influence, but the Word of God is your highest authority.

> *The power of the Word trumps the power of money every single time.*

Having the Word of God on the inside of you means you have life to fuel you, a light and a lamp to guide your way, the unchanging truth to protect you, creative power to promote you, not to mention protection from sin, supernatural provision, healing, and deliverance—just to name a few. Everything you are and everything you will ever be is created and sustained by the Word of God.

#6: Faith in God

Regardless of how much money is in their bank account, everyone on this earth has one thing in common: We all face trials in life.

Some can be resolved (at least temporarily) with money; however, there are those situations where no amount of money can provide an adequate solution. What do you do then? How do you overcome the circumstances that money, power, or prestige can't fix? You must then turn to another one of the Bible's "true riches"—faith in God.

At the onset, having faith in God sounds simple, but allow me to uncover it a bit further. Just because you believe in God is not a guarantee that you have faith in God. I believe that one day, we will have commercial travel to outer space. Does that mean I'm ever going to climb in one of those airships, buckle my seatbelt, and let it take me outside of the Earth's atmosphere? Absolutely not! I believe it, but I don't have faith in it.

Belief and faith are vastly different.

Having real faith in God is more valuable than any amount of money you could ever amass. The Apostle Peter put it like this:

> ". . . that the genuineness of your faith, being much more precious than gold that perishes, though it is tested by fire, may be found to praise, honor, and glory at the revelation of Jesus Christ . . ." —1 Peter 1:7

Just because you believe in God is not a guarantee that you have faith in God.

Whatever the Bible describes as "more precious than gold" should grab your attention. All the gold in Fort Knox could not buy what faith in God—even the size of a mustard seed—could produce. Money might resolve some issues, but faith can move mountains. Money may win you some friends, but faith produces divine favor and promotion.

No matter the size of the storm that may arise in your life, genuine faith in God—not your wealth—will bring you through to the other side. Then, and only then, will you have obtained something which is "more precious than gold." Why spend your time attracting the attention of the world with your wealth when you can bring glory and honor to Jesus through your faith?

That is your real testimony.

LET'S GO!

Life's "true riches"—a relationship with the living God, establishing a good name and reputation, operating in godly wisdom, establishing a strong family, living in God's Word, and having faith in Him—are things no amount of money can buy. And as we've seen numerous times throughout this book, you don't have to exchange "true riches" for material wealth.

You can have both.

This amazing life God has provided is one that recognizes and pursues those things that are fiscally immeasurable and enjoys financial benefits. It really is the good life.

Let's start living it!

chapter 10

THE MISSING LINK

*P*ractically every person I meet wants to live the good life. And why wouldn't they? The thought of not living week-to-week and having a life of joy, peace, and fulfillment, along with having enough resources for themselves and others is welcoming, to say the least. So, what's the holdup? Why aren't more Christians living and enjoying this life of abundance Jesus came to give? What's the missing link?

Two words come to mind: action and diligence.

Derek Sivers, founder and former president of CD Baby, made a great statement when he said, "If more information was the answer, then we'd all be billionaires with perfect abs."[27] We all know it's true, and Christians are not exempt.

---

27 Derek Sivers, "If more information was the answer, then we'd all be billionaires with perfect abs," QuoteFancy, 2023, https://quotefancy.com/quote/2058374/Derek-Sivers-If-more-information-was-the-answer-then-we-d-all-be-billionaires-with

How many believers have heard the principles on how to live the life of their dreams, yet never put them into action? Far too many to count. Does that make what God has promised concerning prosperity and abundance invalid? Certainly not. The Word is true. God never changes. All His promises are "Yes and amen." If they work for some, they will work for all . . .

. . . That is if you work the promises.

BOTH SIDES OF THE COIN

Every coin has two images, sometimes called "heads" and "tails". Without both sides, the coin loses its identity and is considered a counterfeit. To gain the value of the coin, you must have both sides present and working. It's the exact same principle in living the good life.

> *If you want God to move on your behalf, you need to move your behind!*

On one side of this coin is God's provisions—His Word, Spirit, wisdom, strength, etc. On the other side lies another component—YOU! Wouldn't it be nice to finish this book and then sit back and watch God rain down blessings from heaven? Sure, it would. But it doesn't work that way. Living the good life requires more than digesting good information; you must put what you know into practice. The Bible says if you have faith but have no corresponding actions, you're dead in the water (James 2:14). The principle is this: If you want God to move on your behalf, you need to move your behind!

No amount of faith can produce the good life until it's activated and released into your life. Knowledge—knowing what to do—must be transferred in wisdom—doing what you know to do. For example, plenty of Christians know the benefits of tithing, but few apply that principle to their lives. The same is true with the importance of establishing a savings account. Many recognize its value, but some would rather drive a Mercedes (that they can't afford) than have the discipline to put money away each month.

Living the good life is not all dependent upon God. The other side of the coin—you—must be engaged, as well, for blessings to flow and overtake your life.

KNOW THE KEY

During our journey, we've examined many key areas of living in abundance. Things like winning at work, having an "above and beyond" mentality on your job, learning the power of investing instead of spending, placing value on things money can't buy, etc. But I believe of all the practical applications given, one deserves special attention. It's called "diligence", and it's a most crucial element to receiving all God has in store for your life.

To be diligent simply means to work hard at something and stay with it—no matter the obstacles that come your way. Diligence turns talent into fortunes and legacies. Golden State Warrior point guard, Steph Curry, is one of the most accurate three-point shooters in NBA history. Sure, he has talent, but that alone isn't enough. Since junior high, Steph Curry has shot upwards of 500 three-point shots a day. Not one day here or there—practically EVERY day for the last fifteen years.

Diligence is the key!

Persistent, constant hard work pays off. Don't abandon your dreams after one setback or disappointment. Think of where we would be today if Henry Ford, Bill Gates, George Washington Carver, or Otis Boykin (who invented the technology for pacemakers) would have given up. Renowned motivational speaker and author, Napoleon Hill, said:

> *"Effort only fully releases its reward after a person refuses to quit."*[28]

Keep with it. Chart your course and then stay the course.

Over the years, God has blessed me with the opportunity to associate with people of great wealth—both fiscal and "true riches". Some have become dear, lifelong friends while others are casual/business acquaintances. Whatever category of relationship, I've always made an effort to learn and study their habits, routines, and strengths. After years of observation, one common trait resided in all of them: diligence—the relentless tenacity and determination to continually improve their skill and to keep moving forward regardless of the difficulties. Watching how each one pressed for God's best was so inspirational and a much-needed lesson for me to learn.

Even if you don't have much right now, start being industrious. Be eager to learn. Start applying what you've seen, heard, and read. You must start right where you are if you're ever going to get to the place you desire.

---

28 Napolean Hilla, "Effort only fully releases its reward after a person refuses to quite," QuoteFancy, 2023, https://quotefancy.com/quote/145752/Napoleon-Hill-Effort-only-fully-releases-its-reward-after-a-person-refuses-to-quit.

If getting out of debt is your goal, start with the smallest bill and work to pay it off. Then move on to the next one, then the next one, and so forth. Don't wait until you make "x" amount of dollars to tithe. Start now, where you are, and believe God for increase. It's never too early to begin to operate in diligence.

THE BENEFITS

Perseverance is rarely easy, but it does come with some incredible rewards. The Bible says that God is a "rewarder of those who diligently seek Him" (Hebrews 11:6). It's no coincidence that these two root words, "reward" and "diligent," are used in the same sentence. They work in tandem both spiritually and naturally.

The book of Proverbs describes diligence as "a man's precious possession" (Proverbs 12:27). Practicing a life of perseverance places you in a position to reap some incredible benefits. Here's a list of just a few.

> You must start right where you are if you're ever going to get to the place you desire.

Benefit #1: Diligence Gives You an Advantage

Proverbs 21:5 says that the plans of the diligent lead to plenty. I want to draw attention to the word "plans." Notice the Bible doesn't say: "The haphazard life of the inconsistent leads to plenty." People who are diligent make a plan of action and then work hard to make it happen. The old saying is true: "If you fail to plan, you are planning to fail. Plan your work and then work your plan."

Being the leader of staff has allowed me to understand and work with many different personality traits. What I have come to realize is that anybody, regardless of their strengths or weaknesses, can practice diligence in some area of their lives. Let's apply this to your life.

Maybe you're not the most organized person in the world, even to the point that the thought of planning your next day makes you shutter. That's okay. You can still be diligent in your area of expertise and passion. What can you do, every day, to improve? If sticking with a list of five things is too much, then start with three . . . or two . . . or even one. The key is to start where you are, make a plan, put it into action, and stick with it.

Whether you're black, white, brown, employed, unemployed, underemployed, or heading toward retirement, a life marked with diligence will give you an insurmountable advantage over everyone else. Be meticulous, even in the small things that seem insignificant at the time. Your job may determine your income, but your diligence will determine your increase. When you do, get ready to live in the land of "plenty."

Benefit #2: Diligence Gives You a Position

Most Christians have read or heard a message on Deuteronomy 28 more times than they can remember. It's a great chapter chocked full of God's promises to His children. While you may have heard it many times, there's a word in Deuteronomy 28:1 that you might not realize is part of this "blessing" equation. Can you take a guess at what that word might be?

> "Now it shall come to pass, if you diligently obey the voice of the LORD your God . . ."

If you what? Diligently obey—not just casually do what the Word says whenever you feel like it. It sounds a lot like a Scripture we've already seen in Hebrews 11:6—God rewards those who "diligently seek Him." The blessings of God are looking for those who relentlessly pursue Him and His Word. You don't have to necessarily move to another city, state, or country for God to bless you. Be consistent where you are, and watch God honor your diligent pursuit of His Word.

Your job may determine your income, but your diligence will determine your increase.

Living a life of diligence will put you in control of your situations instead of your situations controlling your life. Proverbs 12:24 says that the hand of the diligent will rule. That sounds a whole lot like Deuteronomy 28—that you will be the head, not the tail; blessed in the city and field, blessed in your coming and going, when you rise and when you sleep, etc. Your relentless pursuit of excellence is not going unnoticed. Supervisors are watching. Upper management is watching. Most importantly, God is watching, and that is the greatest reward!

Benefit #3: Diligence Gives Lasting Fulfillment

I want to turn your attention to a very important scripture concerning this subject. This passage should be enough motivation for you to make a commitment to diligence for the rest of your life. Are you ready? Take a look:

> "The soul of a lazy man desires, and has nothing; but the soul of the diligent shall be made rich." —Proverbs 13:4

There is so much truth in this scripture to unpack, but let's focus on a couple of words. First, "desire." Contrary to popular belief, simply desiring a better life is not enough to get you there. Dreams and desires are a start, but to be successful in life, you must be diligent in your execution. Lazy people—better known as "wishful thinkers"—are ones who dream all day and usually end up with nothing. Why? Because wishful thinking alone will never produce anything tangible until it's coupled with exceptional effort.

Yes, the Bible says that God will give you the desires of your heart, but only if you commit your way to Him. Desire is only the beginning; committing to stay with the plan will bring it to pass.

The word "rich" in this scripture is a great word. It denotes an extreme abundance, fulfillment, and overflowing satisfaction that can be enjoyed incessantly, without an expiration date. This relates to both wealth and riches. When you are diligent in your credible desires, your heart will be at ease, God will bless your efforts, and you will live an abundant, fulfilled life.

Nothing could be better.

> *. . . Wishful thinking alone will never produce anything tangible until it's coupled with exceptional effort.*

Benefit #4: Diligence Will Place You in Front of Those with Authority

One of my favorite scriptures on this topic is found in Proverbs 22:29 which says:

> "Do you see a man who excels in his work? He will stand before kings; He will not stand before unknown men."

Anyone who has ever been diligent about their life or business over a long period of time has faced periods of frustration, exhaustion, discouragement, and burnout. I have experienced all of these in my journey—sometimes all at the same time! But look what the Bible says awaits those who stay diligent about their business: that they will stand before those with influence and not common men. This means that when you're persistent, the CEOs of Fortune 500 companies will be searching you out. And when they find you, then the wisdom of God can take over, possibly unveiling a sales strategy that can exponentially increase their profits.

In 1848, thirteen-year-old Andrew Carnegie immigrated from Scotland to America with his family. Trying to help keep his family from starvation, young Carnegie went to work as a telegraph messenger boy earning $2.50 per week. After a few years of diligent work, Andrew was noticed and swiftly promoted, reaching an executive-level position very quickly. It wasn't long before this immigrant boy began investing his savings into the growing steel and railroad industries, which enabled him to leave his employer and build his steel empire. Upon his death in 1919, Andrew Carnegie was considered one of the wealthiest men on the earth—all stemming from a telegraph messenger boy.

Eagerly pursuing your business and personal dreams and desires will require sacrifice. Like I have said many times in this book, start where you are. Instead of binge-watching the latest Netflix craze, invest that time into reading a trade journal, blog, the Bible or listening to a podcast from an expert in your industry. These are not earth-shattering changes, but they can produce significant results in your everyday life and future. A famous doctor once said, "The more that you read, the more things you will know. The more that you learn, the more places you'll go." That was, of course, Dr. Seuss in his classic children's book *I Can Read with My Eyes Shut!*[29]

Are you tired of living at your level in life? Do you desire more? Would you like to gain the attention of someone high up the ladder? Diligence is the key. Get started today. You will be amazed at the results.

Benefit #5: Diligence Provides for Your Needs

Successful people, for the most part, obtained their success by consistently working long, hard hours. The Bible describes this type of work ethic and the benefits thereof in Proverbs 28:19:

---

29 Dr. Seuss, *I Can Read with My Eyes Shut!* (Westminster, MD: Random House Educational Media, 1978).

> "He who tills his land will have plenty of bread, but he who follows frivolity will have poverty enough!"

Simply put: If you work your land, you'll have plenty of bread. But if you fool around, poverty is coming your way.

One of the ways perseverance provides for your needs is through consistent tithing and offering. NOTE: Giving God a tip every other month doesn't qualify you as a tither any more than flossing your teeth the night before your dentist appointment makes you a flosser! God's Word promises supernatural provision, but only to the ones who participate in a steady flow of giving. Even if you find yourself in rock-bottom poverty, never stop the outflow of giving to the Lord.

It's your lifeline to increase and blessing.

When you are diligent in your work and giving (among other things), you're setting yourself up for Almighty God to supply all your needs—not according to your paycheck or salary package, but according to His riches in glory.

Benefit #6: Diligence Brings Profitability

Every business loves to make a profit. Without it, they won't be in business very long. Profitability not only is the bottom line for companies and businesses, but it's also a welcomed companion along your road to success.

To profit means to increase. And who doesn't desire increase, promotion, and blessing? If you're pursuing the good life, you sure do. So, let's find out how to obtain it.

Proverbs 14:23 lays out a great principle for increase:

> "In all labor there is profit, but idle chatter leads only to poverty."

Do you see a word that keeps reoccurring throughout this book? It's the word "labor," a.k.a. "work". Diligent labor brings profit and increase. Sure, there are other things that can bring a temporary increase to your life: gambling, winning the lottery, racking up credit card charges, and cheating on your taxes—to name a few. But these only give an illusion of increase. Yes, you may have more money in the bank if you win the lottery, but those riches are usually short-lived.

A lady in my home state of New Jersey won the state lottery not once, but twice. Her combined winnings totaled over $5 million. Today, due to a gambling habit, loans to family and friends, and bad investments, she's broke.

Diligence in your work habits and the handling of your daily life is only half of the equation to increase. You must, first and foremost, be studious and committed to the Word of God. David put it like this:

> Blessed is the man who walks not in the counsel of the ungodly, nor stands in the path of sinners, nor sits in the seat of the scornful; but his delight is in the law of the LORD, and in His law he meditates day and night. He shall be like a tree planted by the rivers of water, that brings forth its fruit in its season, whose leaf also shall not wither; and whatever he does shall prosper. —Psalm 1:1-3

Just as you can't give an offering every now and then and expect God to bless it, you can't read the Bible once every six months and think God will prosper your life. David gave the pattern to blessing: to meditate on God's Word day and night, and night and day, and day and night. Day after day. Night after night. Over and over again. That's diligence. That's consistency. When you live in the Word and let the Word live in you, supernatural increase and prosperity are sure to follow.

LIVING THE LIFE

Are you ready to begin walking and living in everything God has provided? Are you ready to start living that Ephesians 3:20 life that truly is "exceedingly abundantly above all you ask or think?" Diligence is the key.

> *When you live in the Word and let the Word live in you, supernatural increase and prosperity are sure to follow.*

Ecclesiastes 9:10 says: "Whatever your hand finds to do, do it with your might . . ." Stop being lazy! Get up and get busy. Put a plan of action together and work your plan. Finish your projects. Follow instructions. Do the job right the first time. Put diligence to work for you.

It doesn't matter what your last name is or where you come from; what God has done for others, He will surely do for you. There are two requirements:

> "If you are willing and obedient, you shall eat the good of the land." —Isaiah 1:19

I know you're willing and ready. Applying diligence and obedience to what you have seen and learned will pave the way to a life that will blow your mind. A life that you may not have even recognized exists until now. A life that will bring you fulfillment on every level. What kind of life am I talking about?

THE GOOD LIFE.

Welcome, my friend, to your new way of life!

AUTHOR BIO

LAWRENCE RAPHAEL POWELL is the Senior Pastor of Agape Family Worship Center in Rahway, New Jersey. With over thirty years in ministry, Lawrence is transforming lives with his powerful, prolific, and practical presentation of the Gospel. Thousands of families from across the tri-state region flock to Agape every week to experience warm fellowship, dynamic worship, and anointed teaching. Through outreach, evangelism, and multimedia broadcasting, Lawrence is bringing the Good News of Jesus Christ to people all over the world.

His beginnings were humble when he first answered the call of God to pastor in 1990. The first service was held in his parent's garage in Rahway. He, along with ten others, were in attendance. From a small garage, to the now state–of–the–art facility known as Agape Pointe, Lawrence's vision still remains the same, "to proclaim and demonstrate the love of God to the world." His humble spirit and genuine heart for people endear him to diverse audiences of every ethnicity. With a strong commitment and genuine passion for outreach and evangelism, Agape provides assistance to the local community by supplying resources, materials, and support services. Countless testimonies of hope, healing, and transformation pour in from those being touched and liberated through Agape's outreach efforts.

A much sought-after speaker, respected Biblical teacher, and author, Lawrence earned a bachelor's degree from Rutgers University, a master's degree from Oral Roberts University, and a Doctorate in Strategic Leadership from Regent University. It is obvious to all who know him that he is preparing and positioning a mighty generation of leaders at Agape. It is a generation of world changers, poised to advance and expand the Kingdom for the glory of God. Lawrence is also the doting father of three young adults—Adria Janelle, Aaron Raphael, and Ashlyn Gabrielle.

CONTACT

www.agapecenter.org 732.680.9800

SOCIAL MEDIA

Dr. Lawrence Powell Instagram.com/drlawrencepowell Twitter.com/drlarrypowell

Agape Family Worship Center Instagram.com/agaperahway Facebook.com/agaperahway Twitter.com/agaperahway